"I've had a professional relationship with Tom for many years. The information I've learned from him has been invaluable, and now he's put his knowledge into a book! *Building Wealth, Protecting Dreams* captures Tom's knowledge and practical insight into how he has helped his clients."

—Erich Earhart, mortgage broker

"A sign of wisdom is the ability to learn from your mistakes and successes and also to learn from the mistakes and successes of others. *Building Wealth, Protecting Dreams* is filled with Tom's wisdom and I feel it provides readers with a road map to help achieve financial success. Don't read this book, study it! Apply what you learn, and you too will be able to determine your own financial success. Thanks for your financial wisdom, Tom!

—Kevin Knebl, CMEC, international speaker, author, and trainer

"A fresh and touching perspective on planning for our future. I see this as a must-read when planning for retirement!"

—Rebecca A. Hobbs, Esq., CELA

"This book provides an inspiring education for new and seasoned investors alike. I know Tom to be a very smart financial educator and financial advocate. His approach is particularly insightful because of his great personal and professional integrity and genuine care for his clients."

—Matt Bellis, business owner

"This book is filled with advice that comes right from the heart. Tom's approach to financial planning has a family friendly feel. Similar to a parent, Tom knows how to take care of clients as if they were family members with his warm, caring nature. In my opinion, he is a professional who can deliver the facts to help readers get to the ultimate goal—a secure retirement!"

—Tracy Russo, certified long-term care insurance specialist

"In my view, *Building Wealth, Protecting Dreams* is a must-read for anyone contemplating retirement in the next decade or two. In an entertaining and nonjudgmental fashion, it confronts the myriad of issues younger baby boomers face as they look toward future retirement. The book provides many realistic strategies that readers of any income level looking for a prosperous future will find useful. I highly recommend it."

—Maureen McBride, partner, Lamb McErlane, P.C.

BUILDING WEALTH

PROTECTING DREAMS

BUILDING WEALTH

PROTECTING DREAMS

PURPOSEFUL STRATEGIES TO HELP ACHIEVE
THE RETIREMENT YOU DESERVE

THOMAS A. KALEJTA

Published by Advantage, Charleston, South Carolina.
Member of Advantage Media Group.

ADVANTAGE is a registered trademark, and the Advantage colophon is a trademark of Advantage Media Group, Inc.

Printed in the United States of America.

ISBN: 978-1-59932-769-3
LCCN: 2017934569

Cover design by Katie Biondo.

TreeNeutral

Advantage Media Group is proud to be a part of the Tree Neutral® program. Tree Neutral offsets the number of trees consumed in the production and printing of this book by taking proactive steps such as planting trees in direct proportion to the number of trees used to print books. To learn more about Tree Neutral, please visit **www.treeneutral.com.**

Advantage Media Group is a publisher of business, self-improvement, and professional development books. We help entrepreneurs, business leaders, and professionals share their Stories, Passion, and Knowledge to help others Learn & Grow. Do you have a manuscript or book idea that you would like us to consider for publishing? Please visit **advantagefamily.com** or call **1.866.775.1696.**

To my parents, Thomas and Joan Kalejta, who inspired my passion for helping people; my wife, Susan, for supporting me and believing in my vision; and my children, Ethan and Riley, for making me a very proud father. Without them, this book would not have been possible.

FOREWORD

I was fresh-faced and determined to take over the world, or at least my local town, when I first met Tom Kalejta. I was three years into my professional career and employed by the retail advertising department of my local newspaper. It was a sunny afternoon the day I walked into Tom's office, poised and prepared to make a new account. As chances would have it, Tom was in the market to publish an advertisement that day. He had a financial seminar he would be offering in multiple local schools and he needed to advertise the dates. I gained his business that day, but I never could have known the series of events that would follow.

While taking down the details about the seminar for Tom's advertisement, I became the one intrigued by what he had to offer. And by the time the classes began, I found myself sitting amongst the students in his class that night. Even as a young person, Tom's material was fascinating, albeit totally overwhelming. I realized that night that everyone grows up wanting to make money, but many do not know what to do with it once they have it—other than spend it of course! Tom's seminar was a wake-up call for me, and from the sounds of the other people in the class, many of them felt the same way. During those four weeks, I experienced firsthand Tom's breadth of knowledge and his passion for sharing it with others. I think it was safe to say that we learned more about finances from Tom than any other person—either personal or professional.

That was back in 2006. I took a position working for Tom's firm that summer and never looked back. Fast-forward to 2017, and I've been working with him for over ten years. I've been a part of the firm's growth, and I've personally known all of the clients whose stories he has shared in the pages of this book. I've walked alongside Tom, and I've been an instrumental part in helping him build the firm he has today. I believe this is why he presented me with the opportunity to write the foreword. And for that, I am humbled and grateful.

You might be reading this book right now because someone who knows Tom personally or professionally has shared it with you. That's wonderful and I fully expect that the book will have that kind of effect. For years, clients have been asking me about his seminars and if he still teaches them. The release of *Building Wealth, Protecting Dreams* provides a way for clients and previous seminar attendees to share the knowledge that they learned from Tom all those years ago.

This book is a reflection of Tom's expertise and professionalism. It conveys his personality and his passion for what he does and more importantly *why* he does it! You'll really feel like you know him as he guides you through your quest for purposeful strategies to help achieve the retirement you deserve.

Upon your completion of this book, I think you'll really see that Tom's goal for writing this book was simple—to share his financial knowledge and educate others. That's it. His commitment to his clients is far greater than any other professional motivation. He probably doesn't want to become the next "big financial guru" on radio or TV. He's simply trying to help the average American family increase their chances of achieving their financial goals and dreams.

So much has changed over the last ten years, but no matter how much changes, some things always remain the same. Tom's unwavering commitment to his clients and his focus on financial education has been a core belief since the day I first met him.

From publishing an advertisement in the local newspaper to publishing a book, Tom has come a long way. It's been an exciting journey, and I look forward to seeing the *next* series of events that follow. Thanks for the fun ride, Tom!

—Kristin M. Reeser
Digital Media Coordinator, Kalejta Financial Management

THOMAS A. KALEJTA
CFS®, ChFC®, RFC®, AEP®, CASL®, AIF®

Tom is president and founder of Kalejta Financial Management, founded in 1996. Tom acts as a fiduciary and maintains his highest commitment to the families with whom he does business. Every day, he changes people's lives by helping them to make decisions that will affect their financial futures. Tom specializes in retirement readiness, with a vision for every client to enjoy financial freedom and prosperity. He is committed to empowering every client with the ability to develop purposeful strategies to help build their wealth, protect their dreams, and achieve the retirement they deserve.

Tom's professional designations include: Certified Fund Specialist˚ (CFS˚), Chartered Financial Consultant˚ (ChFC˚), Registered Financial Consultant (RFC˚), Accredited Estate Planner (AEP˚), Chartered Advisor for Senior Living (CASL˚), and Accredited Investment Fiduciary (AIF˚). His bachelor's degree is in marketing and business administration from Penn State University, and he currently holds FINRA Series 6, 7, 26, 63, and 65 registrations. In addition, Tom addresses family and business protection needs by providing life, disability, and long-term-care insurance. He has also been honored with recognition by *Philadelphia Magazine* as a Five-Star Wealth Manager for the years 2009, 2010, 2012, 2013, 2014, and 2015.

Tom is a member of many professional organizations including but not limited to the Collegeville Economic Development Corporation, Montgomery County Estate Planning Council, Perkiomen Valley Chamber of Commerce, National Association of Insurance and Financial Advisors, Institute of Business and Finance, Society of Financial Service Professionals, Financial Services Institute, and International Association of Registered Financial Consultants and is an alumnus of the American College of Bryn Mawr.

Tom and his firm have partnered with Autism Speaks through "Philadelphia Walk Now for Autism Speaks" since 2007. His team, "Ethan's Allies," raises funds every year and often participates in the walk at Citizens Bank Park in Philadelphia. This cause is very close to his heart: His son, Ethan, was diagnosed with autism in 2005.

Tom and his wife, Susan, live in Sanatoga, PA, with their two children, Ethan and Riley. As a family, they love traveling, biking, tennis, and the beach. Tom personally enjoys golfing, fishing, hunting, and gardening.

TABLE OF CONTENTS

THAT'S NOT ME!

I could see the pride in their faces. My mother and father had come to a money management seminar that I was teaching, and I was grateful that they were able to see their son doing what he felt called to do. I wanted them to see not only that I was making it but also that I was helping other people make it. This was my tribute to them.

This was in the late 1990s, a few years after I launched my financial planning business. As they listened intently, I could tell that my parents approved of my new financial planning firm. They saw me helping others grasp the financial concepts that would serve them well for a lifetime. Thomas F. and Joan Kalejta, in their own years together, had their share of challenges. I was determined now to focus on helping families to avoid the common mistakes that so often set them back.

For several years I taught community courses at local schools and colleges as an educational division of my practice. This particular seminar involved nine hours of classroom instruction over three evenings, with advice on building wealth and budgeting, planning for college expenses, buying a house, and the many concerns of the accumulation years. I'm sure those topics resonated with my parents as they thought about their own experiences in raising a family. I wondered if perhaps these were things they wished they had known.

I have come to deeply appreciate the integrity and work ethic that my parents modeled for their family. Ours was a modest, blue-collar household in Pottstown, Pennsylvania. My parents had moved to the Pottstown area from up in the coal regions of Shamokin and Mount Carmel. Dad had been in the army during the Korean War, which led to his trade as a machinist. He was a *MacGyver* sort of guy, able to fix virtually anything around the house, and he shared with me his love of hunting, fishing, and gardening. I will always treasure the memory of my father's company picnics at Dorney Park and our summer trips to Knoebels Amusement Park.

"So are you planning to go to college?" my father asked me when I was about to graduate from high school. I nodded. "Well, good luck then," he said. "We'll help as best we can, but you're really on your own." I got a job that summer at the factory where he worked, and I earned nearly $5,000 to help pay for almost a whole year at Penn State. The experience I gained in working with molten metal and die-cast machines allowed me to appreciate my father's work ethic and hard labor.

I think all parents want their children to have it better than they did. My dad had learned a good trade to make a decent living, and he wasn't working in the coal mines like earlier generations as they struggled to raise their large families. I was the second youngest of four children, and my parents hoped to see us all get through college and have good careers.

In fact, it had been my father's hope to even see us grow up. For almost thirty years, he battled cancer. After a large tumor was found in his stomach when he was in his fifties, he dreamed that he would at least see us all graduate from high school. As it turned out, he saw all of us get our college degrees, and by the time he passed away in 2010, he had six grandchildren.

What he taught me is in my marrow. He was thrifty by nature. Even today, as I manage million-dollar-plus portfolios, I think of my father as I stoop to pick up a penny from the sidewalk. I saw him do that many times, and I saw him clip coupons and bargain for deals at the farmers' market. He supported four kids in a small Cape Cod house on a machinist's salary.

Our mother devoted herself to us, and I saw in her the model of selfless love. She, too, heralded from the coal regions, where she had a difficult childhood. Her father died young, of black lung from his years in the mines, and her mother struggled with alcoholism. Those experiences, I believe, inspired my mother to give her children all of herself that she possibly could. She wanted us to feel the strength of family. It was all about us, never about her. I know that in my own family in the years since, I have tried to follow her example through challenging times.

I learned much about life from my parents and much about money, too—including what not to do with it. Observing my father's mistakes led me to want to incorporate financial education into my career. Dad was cautious with money but experienced a couple of big disappointments. I'll explain later, but I imagine those were on his mind as he listened to me that day at the seminar.

My first job after college was managing a CVS pharmacy. My customers and coworkers kept telling me that I seemed to be a natural at teaching and advocacy and explaining things in a way that people could understand. I had never imagined myself in that role, but that inclination was soon to express itself. Switching to the world of finance, I got a job at a brokerage firm, and I found myself selling mutual funds, annuities, and life insurance. I felt a deep frustration because I wanted to help people plan their lives, not just sell them products.

That desire led me within a few years to found my own firm, and that's why I also began teaching workshops, classes, and seminars so that I might extend that focus beyond my practice and into the community. I did get some teasing from my dad for the amount of time I was devoting to my new business: "Didn't you say that once you were your own boss, we'd have more time to go fishing together? So where's that rod and reel, son?" But I think he knew that I was on the right track. It fit in with his work ethic.

Soon, however, I felt a new sense of frustration: People simply did not understand what I did for a living. At social gatherings, whenever I mentioned my occupation, I could see their eyes glazing over at the words "financial planner," as if that were akin to "used-car salesman." It was certain to shut down the conversation. The stigma was difficult to overcome, even after a decade of teaching and many years in the business. I wanted to cry out, "That's not me—I'm not one of those people!" I wanted them to know that my job was to spend time with families, learn about their goals, and educate them.

It can be hard to break down the natural resistance that some people feel. In my initial talk with clients, I try to help them get past that resistance. One gentleman began our meeting by pushing his chair back from mine and sitting with arms crossed. It took almost an hour, but eventually those arms uncrossed and he slid his chair closer to hear more. He could tell that I was on his side and that we were a good fit. That's what people need to know.

When I was younger, I enjoyed helping educate my peers. As I got into my forties and had been in the business a decade, a lot of my clients were getting toward middle age as well. I sensed that they were starting to see retirement as something not so distant and that I might best be of service now in helping them to avoid a whole new set of mistakes. I began working with them in smaller groups and individually so that I might offer more personal attention, and they could see that I was on their side as well.

In my practice today, I typically work with people who are forty-five to seventy. The younger ones are still building their wealth, but those who are sixty and older are also in the preservation phase and may be in the distribution years of their lives. Through my firm's not-for-profit divisions of the Financial Education Company and the Retirement Resource Center I have taught workshops, classes, and seminars for those who are on the verge of retirement or who have already entered that stage of life.

This is strictly educational. I am not out to sell anything. My planning services are available to attendees if they so desire, but my primary purpose is to spread the word to a wide audience about financial planning practices that can lead to a fulfilling retirement.

And that is why I am writing this book. People work so hard to climb the ladder to earn those raises, bonuses, and promotions. They do not plan for the future, because they get caught up in the moment. They need to be taking stock of what they are doing day by day—investing smartly, saving on taxes, building sufficient resources to retire—but they also need vision. What's the meaning of it all?

It's good to work hard for your money, but your money also should be working hard for you. It should bring you freedom and choices. It's not the money that you need. What you need are the dreams that money can help you achieve. You deserve it!

A LIFETIME OF CARING

Our son, Ethan, developed normally for the first year of his life, but by the time he was two years old he had not made much more developmental progress. My wife, Susan, and I didn't quite know what to make of it.

One afternoon when we happened to be home together, a few stray words from the television caught our attention. It was Oprah Winfrey, cutting for a commercial break, "And when we return, ten signs that your child may have autism . . ."

Sue and I looked at each other, without words, then back at the TV as the program resumed. As we listened to those signs, one after another, it was "check, check, check, check." All of them described our little boy. I looked at Sue again, and she was crying. "That's Ethan," she said.

We took him to a pediatric specialist, and after he finished the examination, he solemnly told us what we already knew. "Yes, doctor, we know it's autism," I said. "We just want to know what's next. What do we do now?"

It's a question, I know, that resonates for so many people for so many reasons at so many times in their lives: What do we do now? What's next? What is the next step? For my family and me, Ethan's autism has been the particular challenge that changed our lives. We had come through much—miscarriages, cancers, funerals, and now this. We wondered if our next child would have autism, too, and whether we should risk that. But even as we wondered, the decision was made for us. Sue gave birth to a baby girl nine months later. At the time of this writing, Riley is twelve years old and doing fine.

Ethan has changed the perspectives of us all. More than ever, I appreciate the example of my mother's selfless nature. Like our parents before us, Sue and I want our children to be the best that they can be. We hope that Ethan might someday live independently and be functional in and a benefit to society. That has become a life focus. We are not looking to launch some national campaign, neither am I looking to change the direction of my practice. We want our children to know just how much they are loved. We want Ethan to have the best of education and therapies, and we want Riley to feel in her heart that our attention to her brother makes her no less special. That is our mission, the cornerstone upon which we build.

Life has a way of surprising each of us. I share our story not because it is particularly poignant, for I know that many families have risen to greater challenges. I now understand how my family's share of adversity has sharpened our focus and shaped our purpose.

Today, in my financial planning practice, I have gained greater empathy for my clients. In the years before Ethan, life was about me and my new bride and my new business and all those many ambitions. Today, when clients speak of their dreams and goals for retirement, and of their disappointments and uncertainties, I can relate to them on a more personal level.

I have no doubt that both Ethan and Riley were given to us for a reason, and I will bring to them the values I learned from my own parents. We all need to get in touch with our values. Individuals need that, businesses need that, society needs that. Sometimes we get a wake-up call. If we trust in our values, then we can endure through life's unforeseen circumstances.

THE BEST YOU CAN BE

Just as I want both of our children to be the best they can be, I also want my clients to experience life as the best it can be, with a clear vision of what they can achieve. Most of them are looking for the answer to a basic question: "Do I have enough money to retire someday?"

They do not want to leave that to chance. They want to know whether they are doing the right things to make it happen. They want to be aware of any mistakes. They recognize the advantage of having a third party look at their situation to see whether they should be taking a different approach.

Whether they have enough will depend upon their expectations and goals, and so that is one of the first areas that we explore. It is from that perspective that we can then look at their savings and investments, their estate and tax situation, their income sources for retirement, their risk management, and the other realms of comprehensive financial planning. Each of those contributors, factors, or elements easily could entail a book of its own, and so we start with the essentials—the main concepts in each area that they simply must understand—and then get down to the details that will matter most to the family.

The average age of my clients is about fifty-four. They have, on average, at least $500,000 in investable assets, and they want to make sure that they are on track. They do not think of themselves that way, but they are wealthy when you calculate the value of their homes, their 401(k) plans and other assets, as well as their life insurance policies and their personal property. They don't realize that they are actually millionaires.

Though they might be quite comfortable financially, they still are concerned for their future. They want to make sure that their accustomed lifestyle can continue into retirement. They come to me because they want a plan and a guide. Retirement planning is my passion and the focus of my practice. Most of my clients are on the cusp of retirement or have recently crossed the line. It is critical at this stage that they understand how very different they must treat their money than they did earlier in life. As I will explain in the pages ahead, if they fail to make that adjustment, their portfolios may be in peril.

When you have gathered together a sizable stockpile for retirement, the prospect that you might blow it becomes increasingly frightening. Many of my clients are feeling that pressure. They know they should be doing something differently, but they are not quite sure what or how. In short, they have come to a startling realization and are now anticipating the next step.

They have made their money because they generally have attained some level of expertise. Perhaps they have been astute at business or possess a skill of high value to others. Most of them have had some experience with leadership, and they know that any strong leader understands the importance of delegation. They surround themselves with people who can help them to accomplish specialized tasks that they could not do on their own. They are more concerned about the big picture. That is one of the principles of success, and that often is the spirit in which my clients seek me out.

As income and assets increase, mistakes become magnified as well. A young person just starting out can make a financial mistake, correct it, and learn from it, without undue harm. When you have attained high net worth, those same mistakes could cost a fortune. You could be sacrificing the security and comfort of the lifestyle that you anticipated. No longer can you shrug it off.

Quite often, a prospective client will want to talk about investments and rates of returns and asset allocations, certainly important matters. In our initial meeting, however, what is most important is for each of us to decide whether we could work well together. If the client seems only interested in finding a stockbroker who could produce some prodigious performance, I explain that that's not my objective. My objective is to help my clients reach *their* objectives, enjoy the retirement that they envisioned, and leave a legacy that they feel is appropriate. And then I try to help them achieve whatever rate of return they need to get there.

In other words, growing their wealth must serve a purpose. When we run the numbers, what is most important is whether they are on track to achieve what they have set out to accomplish. Are they aiming for their best?

My aim is to help people build their wealth and protect their dreams. Both matter. I also help them discover their purpose and uncover their "why." The resources certainly could limit one's goals, but without those goals, what is the point of the resources? I certainly want all of my clients to do well with their investments. And I want them to know why they are bothering to do so.

FLIPPING THE SWITCH

In essence, I help people flip the switch into retirement—although for many, the transition is more like adjusting the speed control since they may still be working to some extent. Either way, they are moving from the accumulation phase of their life, the time of building wealth, into the phase of distribution when they are using it and aiming to protect their money—and their dreams.

Many people do not recognize that there is any switch to flip. They do not see how their strategies must change. It can be hard to move out of the mode of making money. They worked so hard to build that nest egg, and now they are expected to crack it?

And yet that is what it was all about. You are allowed to enjoy yourself in retirement, as long as you do so at an appropriate pace. The specifics and timing of how to accomplish that will be different for every family. Some people retire at fifty-five years old, and others wait until they are seventy. The right choice for you will depend upon your situation.

This calls for rational planning that anticipates the risks along with the rewards so that the money can last throughout your lifetime, perhaps with enough remaining to leave a legacy for your loved ones. As you begin to use your assets, the money must be handled with the utmost care. This calls for a new way of managing the portfolio that weighs those risks and puts them in their proper place.

I help people to see those risks. I help them to recognize what they will be up against during a retirement that for many will last three decades or more. With proper planning and appropriate investing, many people can overcome those obstacles. They can live comfortably without worry, knowing that they have enough set aside for the emergencies and contingencies that we all face at one time or another.

In general, some money must be kept accessible and liquid, while other money can be invested for healthy gain and to offset inflation. How much for each purpose? We find out by getting to know you. A guaranteed income might be right for some clients, while others can look for more market opportunities. For most, the right approach will be a combination of strategies, depending on the intended uses for the assets and how soon they will be needed. We will take a closer look at those income strategies in chapter 9.

My two decades of experience have gotten me to the point where I can fairly quickly assess people's financial situation to determine whether they are ready to retire with their desired lifestyle. This is not just a gut feeling. I back up that impression by running two types of financial planning programs. I must be able to tell my clients more than, "I think you can do it." I must be able to tell them, "Yes, you can do it, and here's why."

This is not a time for guessing. Retiring is exciting to anticipate, but once you have made that choice it is generally not an option to change your mind and go back to that high-paying job. In fact, many people have found themselves forced out of their higher-paying jobs when they are in their fifties and sixties, with younger workers taking their place. Once you retire, you can say good-bye to the working world. The finality of the decision means that it is essential that you know for sure that you are financially ready for that step.

I certainly don't beat around the bush. I tell people what I think. It might be this: "Yes, you are on track, congratulations." But it might be this: "I'm sorry, but the way you're doing things is not going to get you to where you want to be at retirement." Or even this: "Unless you're willing to make some changes, I don't think I can help you."

COME WHAT MAY

I wear many hats. Not only am I a financial advisor and planner, but I also feel that I am part accountant, part psychologist, part counselor, and in some ways part attorney. Some days I even provide marriage advice, college selection guidance, and vacation suggestions. In all of those roles, I am helping people to get to where they really want to be. I help them to see how the various elements of their lives interrelate.

Whichever hat I wear, I want my clients to feel confidence in my advice, knowing that my arm is on their shoulder even as I tell them frankly what they need to do or to stop doing. If we can communicate with such openness and honesty and say hello and good-bye with a firm handshake or a hug, I know we have the kind of relationship that works for the long term, whatever happens to them.

Success is what you make of it. Life is about preparing for the challenges and adjusting to them along the way. Once, I felt that my path was to grow my business and raise my family, providing our children with a great college education and someday retiring to sip a mai tai on the beach as the waves came in. For me and my family, the path has turned, and our view has broadened. As we built, the dream shifted—and so now we build anew.

As a professional planner, I have long helped many other families build and adjust to their own needs. When Ethan came into our lives, I was already equipped with the financial knowledge that my own family would require to face this awesome responsibility. It felt as if I were being prepared for the eventuality that Sue and I may be sending only our daughter off to college. Our son may be living with us for the rest of our lives. He needs a lifetime of care. So do we all, in our own way, and I am honored to do what I can to help people along the path of life.

CHAPTER 1

NEW HORIZONS

It was not a traditional wedding ceremony. The bride danced and twirled her way up the aisle to lively music, greeting her groom. It was an atmosphere of rebirth—and a reminder of the limitless possibilities that life can hold for us, if we keep the right attitude.

I had known Natalie for years. She and her former husband had been longtime clients of my financial planning practice, and I had helped them prepare for their future—but it was a future together that was not to be. They generally seemed fine as a couple, but they had a variety of marital and family issues that they could not resolve. They eventually divorced. He chose not to continue working with me, but she still sought my advice. It was a dreary time in her life. She was often downcast.

Many times, the heavy weight of divorce is a severe setback for both parties. In this case, though, I soon witnessed Natalie becoming much more positive, energetic, and outgoing, as if she had been freed from chains. She and her children moved to another state. She kept in touch and remained my client along the way, and with determination and focus, she turned her life around. I was pleased to serve as her coach and guide. And one day, my wife and I got an invitation to her wedding in Florida.

In recent years my focus has switched to helping people to deal with life's complexities as they prepare to retire. Often when they come to see me, some triggering event has prompted them to get financial advice—a death or a birth in the family, a job loss or change of career, or a big inheritance. Sometimes a spouse has passed away and many details must be sorted out. Maybe a family squabble must be resolved before everyone loses out. Often it's a couple just trying to figure out what comes next, now that the nest is empty.

I have worked with analytical types who just want to review figures, but generally I quickly hear about some family situation. Something has prompted the individual or the couple to seek an experienced professional. The underlying concern is: "We don't think we can handle this on our own anymore." They have been experiencing a financial symptom, and they do not want to just treat that symptom anymore, they want to treat the problem. They need some real advice. And that's what opens the conversation as we look at the wide range of family issues that play upon the finances, for better or for worse.

NEW VIEWS OF RETIREMENT

You may recall, just before the turn of the millennium, those television commercials put out by the big brokerage houses. They would show smiling older folks under floppy hats at the beach, sipping drinks with little umbrellas in them, toasting their retirement while gazing at a stunning sunset. We haven't been seeing too many commercials like that since the tech bubble burst soon thereafter and countless portfolios took the plunge. Nor did we see them during the housing crisis and the steep recession later that decade.

The prevailing view of retirement seems to have changed in the twenty-first century. Many have come to realize that it may not be a stroll on the beach. Although that could be the ideal situation for some, it may not be everybody's preference or within their means. Ideally, my wife and I would like a "stroll-on-the-beach" retirement if we can, just like the cover of the book. Our stroll, however, may include our son Ethan with us. For others, it may mean working a little longer than anticipated or perhaps taking a part-time job for a while—hopefully something pleasant without stress. Even among those who have not felt the financial pressures, however, attitudes have been changing. They are seeing retirement as a time, perhaps, to volunteer and do charity work or to go back to school. They might want to start a foundation or travel the world. Or they might just want to spend more time with the children and grandchildren. In any case, they are not necessarily thinking about a beach lounge—at least not every day. Life remains busy, usually for the best. Societal attitudes have changed.

At the personal level, attitudes naturally tend to change when people get into their fifties or sixties and realize that they are closing in on the end of their working years. That longtime career will not continue forever. At some point, maybe very soon, they will be entering this new world called retirement. In one way or another, it will be a significant change in lifestyle—and that calls for mental preparation. The prospect, to some, feels intimidating.

I talk to clients about that very subject. Sure, their financial plan might say they can take that step. On paper, retirement is a go. In reality, maybe not. I want to talk to them about their goals and about their needs, wants, and wishes. How do they feel about this? Can they envision themselves, going about their day-to-day lives, without heading to the workplace? Do they see themselves pursuing dreams? In other words: Is this truly what they want, and are they ready for it? Once they finish work that last Friday, are they prepared to not return on Monday morning?

This is one of life's major decisions, and it must not be made impulsively. That's what brings people to my office doorstep. They understand the need to seek out financial guidance. At this milestone, they want to be sure they are taking everything important under consideration, and that calls for the impartial perspective of somebody who has helped many others just like them.

For one thing, many people feel uneasy inside, though outwardly they may cheer at the prospect of not having to go back to the old grind. Their career has been a lifelong endeavor. Their job has been a major part of their identity. The company has been their lifeblood. They made lasting friendships in the workplace, and they won't be seeing those friends every day now. We sometimes talk about such matters. How will they continue in those relationships when their lifestyles have now changed dramatically? And then there's that paycheck—once they have cleaned out their desk or locker, they won't be getting a regular salary anymore.

How will it go on the home front? Spouses must adjust to this new routine. They may find that all this new togetherness is not always as romantic as they might have expected. What will they do with this newfound time: Will they travel, cultivate a new hobby, or spend more time visiting their children and grandchildren? These domestic considerations and adjustments can be all the more challenging when combined with those ambivalent feelings of leaving the workplace and losing that identity. The thrill of retirement can turn to a chill. It helps to talk through such matters. If you are prepared for such contingencies and know that these are common adjustments, then you will be better able to address them and to adapt.

At age fifty now, I am thinking about such matters myself—and I think about the hundreds of families whom I have helped along the way and the thousands of people whom I have advised. I remember talking with clients about the birth of their children. Then we talked about college graduations and the grandchildren coming along. Now we are talking about their journey into retirement. I have been with them through two decades or more of their progression through the stages of life, and I feel very connected to them. I do not wish to say good-bye to those connections, and I imagine myself someday staying involved though I might be retired. Even if that just means I remain an old friend, I can't just walk away. My career has been a central part of my life, and I understand how it feels when your job is part of your identity.

The best is yet to come, to borrow a phrase. In retirement, some of life's finest years are beginning, and you have the perspective and wisdom that your younger version probably lacked. As you prepare for retirement, you should be anticipating an active and vigorous lifestyle because that has become the norm. Yes, you must plan carefully and you will need time to adjust—and once you do, your dreams await.

PLAYING TO WIN

Certainly, the concerns of life as you near retirement are far different than they were when you were twenty or thirty years old. Then, you were building. You had your high school diploma, perhaps a college degree, and your thoughts soon turned to marrying, buying a house, raising a family, and putting the kids through college. You wanted the American Dream.

The most expensive years of life tend to be in the midforties, when people have the most toys, so to speak. They want the nice cars, the RV, the snowmobile, the jet ski, the boat, and the vacation home. At the same time, they are revving up to get the kids through college. Unfortunately, often there never seems a convenient time to start putting enough money away for retirement. At first, young people tell themselves that retirement is forty years away. Then it's thirty years away, then twenty, then ten—and boom! They wake up one day to an empty nest and they are tired of those toys and they are at the doorstep of retirement. And they're not ready.

The lucky ones wake up early enough. There is so much they can accomplish if they just get started while there is time. Time is the biggest asset of youth. Through the power of compounding over many years, time can turn modest savings into a considerable sum. As the years go by, it loses its power to work that magic in the retirement portfolio. It needs to be left alone to grow, and grow again, before it is ever tapped. For young people, those investments for the most part can be more adventurous, more risky, more oriented toward that growth because time is on their side.

When you are about to retire, you have lost that time advantage. Your focus now must be more oriented toward protection and preservation so that you can distribute your savings over the course of your remaining lifetime—and that could be quite a good while, indeed. It is not that you are out of time. It is that you must be so much more aware of it. Strategies of the accumulation years no longer work as well. They can backfire on you. Generally, this is a time to become more conservative financially—but not too conservative. You still need healthy growth to overcome inflation and to handle life's uncertainties.

If life were a football game, you would be past halftime and back in the action for the second half. The clock is running. You want to get to that goal line, and all the players on your team must be doing their best. You need a good coach, and you need a good playbook.

Football teams often script the early plays. Families do that, too. Parents raise their children and send them out into life with instructions on what they should do—and it is up to them to do it well. They head out to the field of play, but the script only gets them so far. They must strategize and adapt. They must look for opportunities and keep out of trouble. They must maintain a good offense and good defense.

They play hard, and at halftime they reassess the strategy. Should they try to run out the clock or press on? If they have scored well in the first half, they will want to hold that advantage against the forces that would take it away from them. They cannot expect to coast to victory. A few trick plays, and they could lose the game. The strategy changes in the second half. It changes not only because time is of the essence but because so much has happened to rewrite the script.

In the run-up to retirement, many people feel that they are in a catch-22. If they have waited too long to save, they feel caught between the need to handle their money more conservatively and the concern that they are so far behind that they need to take more risks in their financial lives. That's how it feels when time is no longer on your side. Young people may feel they lack the resources or income to save for retirement. Unfortunately, by the time they do have the resources and income, they lack the time. They are too close to retirement. To avoid that catch-22, you have to do your best to find the right balance along the way. "A journey of a thousand miles begins with a single step," said Lao Tzu. If you're fortunate, you take the important first steps toward retirement early in the game.

"People don't plan to fail," the old saying goes, "they fail to plan." No sports team would dream of trying to compete without having practiced and developed a strategy for both the game and for the season. They would not head out without the appropriate equipment. Why, then, would anyone try to play the game of life without the right strategies, equipment, and coaches?

You won't be winning every time. Much of your success will result from how you react to the inevitable losses along the way. Will you be back in the game, more determined than ever? If you have a plan, then you can make it. If you regularly review and revise that plan and are willing to adapt, then you will have the best chance of winning.

CHAPTER 2

WHY BOTHER?

Imagine you are attending an annual business meeting in which none of the principals in attendance has a plan, written strategy, goals, benchmarks, projections, system of measurement, means of accountability, or anything of the sort. Nobody is thinking about the numbers.

Is that the way you would run a business meeting? My guess is that you would insist that everyone take a hard look at those numbers and adjust course accordingly, working toward developing goals for the coming year and an overall vision and strategy for the company. And you would want them to do more than just talk about it. You would require a written business plan with clear objectives and lines of responsibility.

You probably have worked for a business or have owned one yourself. If you understand how foolish it would be to simply ignore the basic functions of a business, would it not make sense to apply those principles to your own family? Wouldn't it make sense to meet regularly with a financial advisor to review how well you have done in the past toward meeting goals and what may need to change? Wouldn't you want specific written objectives that are measurable and, hopefully, attainable?

The steps toward business success are similar to the steps toward personal financial success. Unfortunately, in many families, the state of planning resembles that opening scenario. It is as if they are playing the game of Life, spinning the wheel to see what will happen. From year to year they leave it all to chance, never setting family goals and taking concerted action to attain them.

> "TWO CLASSES OF PEOPLE LOSE MONEY; THOSE WHO ARE TOO WEAK TO GUARD WHAT THEY HAVE; THOSE WHO WIN MONEY BY TRICK. THEY BOTH LOSE IN THE END." —**HENRY FORD**

GOALS FOR A LIFETIME

This calls for reflection. A family, like a business, needs to take the time to ponder these matters. What is our purpose? What is our vision and mission? What are our central values? What goals will we set for ourselves?

In our first meeting, I talk with clients about those fundamental questions. Their answers will have everything to do with the nature of their financial planning and the continuing decisions that they will be making. However, I do sometimes encounter reluctance to talk about setting goals. Some people treat them as New Year's resolutions. The novelty dwindles, and soon they return to their old habits after only a few months. That's the attitude that they bring to goal setting—"Sure, we'll try it, but we are going to fail." It becomes a self-fulfilling prophecy.

Instead, we should be looking long term. What are their needs, wants, and wishes throughout retirement and throughout the rest of their lives? This isn't about losing a few pounds to look good at the beach next summer. And this isn't just about bulking up the portfolio. This is about identifying the ultimate reasons to lose those pounds and to build that wealth. When you know why you are doing something, you are far more likely to do it.

I'm sure you have heard it all before. There's a reason for that. This is important stuff. As a financial planner, I cannot gloss over this. In working with many clients, I know that they come to understand and appreciate why we focus on these fundamentals. In our early discussions together, we unearth dreams. Some clients come to me able to talk with crystal clarity about where they are going and why. Most have not reached that point—but they do get there, and when the pieces fall into place, attitudes change and the real work begins.

When the goals are realistic and measurable, we can put in place the specific financial strategies that will be needed to help attain them. We must start with the big picture. Where are you going? Unless you know, you will be spending a lot of time on dead ends and detours, and you could end up anywhere on the map or stuck in a ditch on a desolate road—because who knows? You certainly don't. It is not the kind of adventure that most people would seek out.

Many people think of financial planning as some assortment of investment strategies, and they may shy away from it because they either do not understand it or they find it intimidating or downright boring. Mostly that translates to the fear of the unknown, which is why I have focused so long on education and advocacy. Knowledge conquers fear. Some people do come to me filled with self-confidence, but a great many really could use a big hug and the assurance of "come on, we can do it." You have to begin. Forgive the cliché, but it is true—the first step of any journey is the hardest.

Certainly what I do involves investments, but it's so much more than day-to-day money management. It includes the broader topics of estate and tax planning strategies, retirement income planning, and the many aspects of risk assessment. If that sounds boring, let me put it this way: what I do involves helping people to manage life. We are not going to get bogged down in details about taxation, investments, rates of return, and revocable trusts. Those are important and some people do find the details to be fun, but what is critical is making it to your destination.

"HOW DO WE MEASURE UP?"

Often, when I have begun working with a couple on their retirement plan, they will ask me how they compare with others with whom I have worked. How are they doing on the financial scale? "How do we measure up?" they ask.

I can only tell them that it's relative. It depends on expectations, goals and dreams, family situation, health, and their desire to leave a legacy—no simple answer is possible. I fully understand, though, why they would want to know. It's a human need. We all want reassurance that we have done all right and that we will be okay.

Sometimes I relate to clients the tale of one of the worst financial situations that I have come across. Melanie and Bob, in their fifties, once came in to meet with me, and when we sat down to look at their financial situation, their net worth was negative. I don't see a negative net worth very often, particularly among people who believe they are on track. This couple had a few hundred thousand dollars in credit card debt, and they figured they should be taking some kind of action to better position themselves for retirement.

They figured right. The financial planning would have to wait. First we had to talk about the elephant in the room—and that was their huge debt. How did this happen?

They said they didn't know. Whenever an expense came up—groceries, vacation, college tuition, whatever—they just charged it. When the credit card bills came in every month, they made the minimum payment, or maybe a little bit more, and carried the balances forward. They didn't pay attention to whether their income supported their lifestyle. They just let it snowball. They had no budget. They had no plan. As the snowball got bigger, they tried not to look at it. It got to the point where their situation was nearly unmanageable.

We had a long talk. I put it delicately, but I explained that what they needed might be more debt management than financial planning. Often, such financial straits point to a psychological issue. Sometimes it is a medical or behavioral problem. It might be an addiction—alcoholism, for example, or gambling. I did not know whether that was the case for them, but I suspected something was behind their debt. "I don't know" just won't do.

Serious issues must be identified and addressed before we can think about retirement planning. We did talk about the basics of how to get credit cards under control, but we also broached the possibility that they might pursue personal or couples counseling as well as debt management counseling. They agreed that they should work on some things and then come back—but I never saw them again.

I am pleased to report that I can tell virtually any couple who comes to see me that they are doing better than that, although many certainly need help. Few are in as good shape as the multimillionaire couple I met who likewise didn't give much thought to retirement. They knew that it would happen someday, but they saw little need to plan for it. Not many people are that financially secure, and even those with plenty of assets may not feel that security. They still wonder if they are doing the right things. Multimillionaires still may not have enough money. We consider ultra-high-net-worth individuals to have $10 million or more. Even at that level there may be things that keep them up at night.

Of course, the more money you have, the more complications you tend to face in estate planning and business transition with high-level finances. It is often said that worries increase with net worth, and they sometimes do. It is more the case, though, that affluent people advance to a different level of planning. They are just picking through a different basket of issues. If given the choice, most people would choose that basket. Most of my clients have a level of wealth that is significant but more modest than that. They are somewhere in the middle.

If you ask me to compare you with others, I might be able to show you some demographics on age and income and educational background to see where you fit—but rest assured, you will be somewhere between those two scenarios I described. I can do a lot for couples in the middle, which means I can do a lot for virtually anyone contemplating retirement, specifically mass-affluent and high-net-worth individuals. Mass affluent have a net worth of about half a million to $2 million and high net worth have $2 million to $10 million.

I do a whole lot more than juggle numbers. Life is more than a portfolio or a trust fund. I care about my clients, and if I see underlying issues I will not hesitate to try to get them to the surface. That's the kind of relationship that I want, and I know that is the kind of relationship that my clients need. Good financial planning does more than identify and treat symptoms. It diagnoses conditions and looks for treatments.

SETTING YOUR PRIORITIES

Those who develop a vision for their retirement are far more likely to feel contented as the years go by. For most people, knowing what they want and seeing real progress toward getting there is enough. They are able to pause and enjoy the scenery along the way.

It's a matter of organizing your life priorities. Why do you have this money? How will you use it, and what do you want to accomplish? Are there places you wish to go, things you hope to learn and do? Who and what are important to you, and do you want to help them? Do you plan to leave money to family or charity?

Again, it comes down to knowing your dreams and goals and envisioning how you would like to be remembered. Most people do not think about these matters before launching into financial planning. Couples do not talk about them. My job is to be the catalyst and facilitator for such discussions before we get very far into any specifics.

This is often new to people. Seldom are words like these spoken in a household: "Honey, let's turn off the TV tonight and silence our smartphones and talk about what we want to accomplish in life. Let's get a grip on what makes us feel happy and fulfilled." Couples might not talk much about it, but each of them probably has given some thought to these bigger issues. I try to draw it out of them. I try to get them to compare their views. It's important to get it out into the open so that we can develop a cohesive plan that both find acceptable and exciting.

We also need to make sure that both spouses are being realistic about what their accumulated resources can do for them. Most dreams come with some sort of cost—and that was the point of all those years of saving. We just need to verify that the resources are in alignment with the aspirations.

Some people have bought into the notion that they should be able to take out 10 percent each year from their accounts. They have heard, perhaps, that the stock market over time performs that well, and they figure that they will do that well, too. In short, it doesn't, and they won't. They are not thinking about volatility, sequence of returns, inflation, fees, and the human tendency to use less-than-perfect judgment. We will be looking at a lot of those variables later in this book.

A number of surveys have asked people how much they thought would be a reasonable rate of withdrawal annually from their retirement account. Most of the answers range from a low of 5 percent to a high of 15 percent. A good advisor in the industry would tell you that a more realistic figure would be 3 or 4 percent. Sometimes, people's perceptions of what they can do are unrealistic. It would be folly to make the decision to retire based on bad information.

In chapter 9, we will take a closer look at the principles of income planning for retirement. For now, let me just say that we can work out the balance sheet to determine whether you are in a position to finance your dreams. Together, we can make sure that you are aiming toward tangible goals that are meaningful to you. You won't be retiring into a vacuum. You will be retiring into some of the best years of your life, and you want to be well equipped on that journey.

ORGANIZING THE DOCUMENTS

Think back for a moment to that absurd scenario in which the company officers around the conference table failed to develop a sensible business plan. They seemed to care nothing for the numbers by which they could measure and project and plan. I'm sure you would insist on a much higher level of competence.

All this talk about the importance of dreaming and establishing your life priorities is not meant to discount the importance of tracking your numbers and monitoring your progress. Yes, you need to get your life in order. And you also need to get your financial house and paperwork in order. In the digital age, "paperwork" may sometimes seem an old-fashioned term, but by whatever means, your documents need to be readily accessible and sensibly filed.

What if a company didn't know what its revenues were or its expenses or profit margin? What if it had no clue about its assets and liabilities? What if it didn't have a balance sheet? Suppose it didn't bother to file its taxes every year. Suppose it just let its debts keep building without refinancing. Would you want to invest in that company? I think you would agree that it has organizational issues.

I help my clients get organized. They worked hard to build their income, resources, and careers. I want to make sure that they are paying attention to what happens to that money. And the way to do that is to examine the documents and keep them close at hand for easy and regular reference. Unless you keep track of these matters, how can you hope to retire someday and achieve your goals?

In our practice we use cloud-based financial planning websites and programs to keep all your finances organized. You need to know at least the basics about the assets that you own, your debt, and what you are spending. You need to be able to see your cash flow. And beyond that, you need to know that your estate planning is in order with all the necessary documents properly in place.

Whether you keep your files on paper in a fireproof safe or tucked away in the cloud somewhere, you need to let somebody know what you are doing. Ideally, your financial planner will have copies— but your loved ones need to know who your financial planner is. I once dealt with a husband who, despite my urging, did not want to trouble his wife about any of their financial affairs. And then he died. She eventually found my business card among his papers. The lesson there is that both spouses must be involved in the family financial planning and that someone needs to know whom to contact and the basics of what to do.

For our first discussion, I do not require people to bring in any of those documents or statements. If they do set a thick pile on my desk, I slide it aside and thank them for their trouble. "We'll get to these eventually," I say, "but I want to know more about you guys first."

Then we begin talking about a wide variety of other matters: How do they view money? What is important to them about it? What do they need and want their money to achieve? Who controls the household finances? Is one spouse a spender and the other a saver? Do they see eye to eye? I find out their story, get a feel for their personalities, and talk about their goals. Only then might we take a look at some of the documents—but first we want to have a pretty good idea of whether we would be a good fit for working together.

THE BIGGEST CAUSE OF FAILURE

The biggest step is getting started. "Action is the foundational key to success," said Pablo Picasso. Time gives you options, but many people put off talking about these matters. Procrastination steals the time that is so precious in making headway in financial planning. It's a robber of wealth.

Why do people postpone such important discussions? Having such important discussions can be difficult. We are talking about the big issues in life—not just the joyous goals but also the troubling challenges. Along with anticipations come trepidations, and somehow it always seems better to talk about troubles tomorrow rather than today. Many people also have misgivings about the decisions they have made in life and are not eager to rehash them. They may feel overwhelmed, but problems postponed tend to worsen. Outdated beneficiaries on a retirement plan or an insurance policy can become a nightmare.

You could point to so many reasons that people fail financially—an overload of bad debt, the lack of an estate plan, poor tax management, a negative attitude, an absence of clear goals. Many would say that poor investments are to blame or the failure to get a high enough rate of return. None of those match the magnitude of the number-one reason. In fact, all of those together are less significant than the chief reason that people fail. *They fail because they procrastinate.*[1]

My job is to get people to move the needle. I encouraged them to get started while they still can make a significant difference. Even if they begin modestly, they get into the habit of saving regularly and they get out of the bad habit of procrastinating. They have taken the hardest step.

Once your financial plan is underway, then all of those other important considerations have a chance of falling into place. Your investments matter. You want to make sure that you choose appropriate ones. I can assure you, though, that you will never have to worry about picking a bad investment if you never get around to picking any investments at all. The best route to success is to resolve to take action today. Then, we can get those actions into the proper order, establishing meaningful goals while staying on course in a concerted effort to meet them.

---

1   Voya Services Company, *Financial Strategies for Successful Retirement* [seminar and workbook], 2017.

CHAPTER 3

PAYING FOR THE AMERICAN DREAM

It's a question that I have heard many times throughout my career, "Should we pay off the mortgage on the house before retiring?" For generations, families have treated their home as an investment, and for many it is one of their largest assets. They wonder how it fits into the equation for retirement planning.

"We have decided that we are going to accelerate our mortgage payment," I frequently hear from clients. Generally, this question comes in the several years just before retirement, when the kids are out of college, asset levels are increasing, and income is strong. "It's kind of making us nervous, having those payments, and we want to see the house become ours, free and clear, by the time we're sixty-five." And my response generally is, "Okay, I understand what you're saying, so let's take a look."

The American Dream of owning your own home lives on. Despite the troubling housing crisis of the last decade, people in general feel a greater sense of security than they did in, say, the Great Depression when the banks would call loans and seize houses unless the hapless homeowners paid in full. Times have changed, and regulations have evolved.

29

Attitudes evolve, too. In our generation, people take varying views toward the role their house plays in their financial well-being. Many people hold to the opinion that it is a great idea to pay off the mortgage before retiring. Many others do not see it that way at all. Whether it's a good idea or a bad idea is not my point here, since that will depend upon the family's situation and perspective. As always, however, it is important to understand all of the options.

GOOD AND BAD DEBTS

The question to consider in paying off the mortgage is how that debt is influencing your financial situation. I view debt as one of three types: good debt, necessary debt, and bad debt.

Bad debt serves no purpose in advancing your financial situation. Credit card debt is a prime example. You cannot deduct the interest from your taxes, and you pay a high interest rate to carry it. Necessary debt might be a loan for a car or something else that you cannot do without, even though the debt is not working in your favor.

By contrast, a good debt is working for you by advancing your potential for a higher net worth. Can there be such a thing? Good debt? Possibly. It may be tax deductible and carries a reasonable interest rate. A mortgage or home equity loan or line of credit can be good debt if the property increases substantially in value. A student loan that enhances your income potential can be a good debt because it might pay for itself in multiples over time.

Some well-known money management thought leaders do not view any kind of debt as good, and others reject debt for religious reasons. I believe it is more a matter of which kind of debt you are dealing with. If you have been an employee or owner of a company, consider whether it owes any money for anything. Does it borrow toward inventory or to invest in research and development? Does it have a line of credit to provide operating flexibility? Suppose your company decided it would spend no more of its revenue on R&D, dividends, raises, infrastructure investment, or even inventory and payroll until every cent of debt was paid. How do you think the stockholders and employees might react?

Most people would predict that the company would collapse. You can be sure that any successful, growing company with a vision for its future carries debt in some form. Such companies do not insist on paying off all of their debt before saving and investing and strategizing. My point is this: Should you?

We hear so much about the government's debt, and those trillions of dollars certainly should give us pause—but would it serve us well if the politicians decided to pay it all off before doing anything else? No more Social Security checks or defense spending or infrastructure repairs until all the national debt is repaid? You might argue the political wisdom of this expense or that, but overall you probably would concede that without the ability to carry debt, the country, like that company, would collapse.

This is not to glorify debt. This is to point out that debt is integral to our society and an essential consideration of comprehensive financial planning. The plan should not necessarily be to eliminate it but rather to eliminate the bad debt, limit the necessary debt, and make the best use of good debt where possible. In their financial planning, people should be considering whether the mortgage on their house qualifies as good debt.[2]

---

2   Voya Services Company, *Financial Strategies for Successful Retirement* [seminar and workbook], 2017.

EXAMPLES OF
TYPES OF DEBT

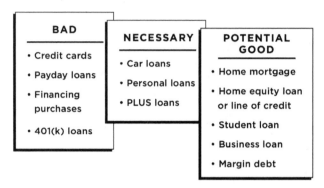

BAD	NECESSARY	POTENTIAL GOOD
• Credit cards	• Car loans	• Home mortgage
• Payday loans	• Personal loans	• Home equity loan or line of credit
• Financing purchases	• PLUS loans	• Student loan
• 401(k) loans		• Business loan
		• Margin debt

HOUSE RICH, CASH POOR

Many people put forward as a goal that they will have their home paid off by the time they retire. Certainly that can be a good idea for some. Others should think twice. I have seen many couples retiring as "house rich but cash poor." They own their house, yes, but they lack sufficient money in their other investments to generate a sufficient retirement income. They end up selling that house, or in some way taking money out of it, as with a home equity loan or reverse mortgage.

In talking this matter through with people, I ask them whether they believe the equity in their home produces a rate of return for them. "Let's say your house is worth $300,000, and you have $100,000 of equity in it," I ask. "Does that $100,000 produce a return?" Generally, they will assure me that its return will be the rate by which the value of the home grows. If it gains 4 percent in value, so does the equity, they say.

"Well, suppose your neighbor also owned a $300,000 home but had no equity in it. Each of your houses gains 4 percent in value. That means you now have a $12,000 gain—but so does your neighbor. How is that fair, considering you have paid off a third of your house and he has paid off none of his? What happened to your equity? Wasn't it working for you?"

I explain that it wasn't the $100,000 in equity that grew. It wasn't the equity that produced the return. It was the value of the home that grew and produced the return. The neighbor made just as much of a gain with zero equity. That example often helps people to understand that perhaps the equity in their home isn't the best place to have their cash.

I offer another scenario. Let's say you have paid off your $300,000 mortgage, but your neighbor still owes $200,000 on his. Because your neighbor didn't spend so much money in house payments over the years, he has been able to put aside several hundred thousand dollars in investments. Now, suppose both your houses dropped in value, as we all know can happen. All your money is in the house, so you've lost a big chunk of it. Meanwhile your neighbor still has all his investments on the side.

Now let's say you both lose your jobs. Your neighbor can tap his other investments for living expenses and to keep up the mortgage payments while he finds another job. Your money is all tied up in your house. Without a job, how will you make the payments? You might think you could ask the bank for a home equity loan, but you're not going to get one when you put down on the application that you are unemployed. It's your equity, but you can't tap into it. You have no wiggle room—you're house rich but cash poor.

Suppose a broker offers you a $300,000 investment. "I guarantee you that your principal will never grow a penny," he says. "It could go down in value, though. If you ever need this in an emergency, you can't touch it. And by the way—no tax advantages." I don't think you would be writing a check to that broker. But what I just described could describe the equity in your home, if you are thinking of it as an investment.

Those are just some thoughts to ponder for those who feel determined that they must pay off the mortgage before they can retire. I try to get people to see that if they have assets in other places, they can always pay off the mortgage if they so choose, or they can use those assets to make the mortgage payments. What they want to avoid is retiring with the bulk of their money tied up in the house and not enough money for their other needs. They should not be in a position where they have to take the money out of the value of their house in order to retire.

SHOULD YOUR HOUSE GO TO COLLEGE?

A common question I have heard repeatedly through the years is this: "Should I borrow against the equity in my house as a way to send my kids to college?" This is one of a variety of ways in which people see their accumulating equity as a ticket to better things—and they figure the more of that equity, the better. They ask about refinancing from a thirty-year mortgage to a fifteen-year one. They ask if they should be sending in additional mortgage payments. They wonder if it would make sense to buy an investment property by borrowing against the value of their house. I address such questions regularly.

James and Wendy were expecting to use the equity in their home to pay for their children's college education in several years. They planned to pay off their mortgage, refinancing it from a thirty-year to a fifteen-year term and then prepaying as much as they could. They figured that would free them from the mortgage payment so that they could afford the tuition along the way. If they needed more, they would get a home equity loan or line of credit. And that was their college plan.

"Well, that's one way to do it," I said, "but think about this a second." I explained that equity in a home produces zero interest. In the meantime, they would be slowly eliminating a big tax deduction, the home mortgage interest. Meanwhile, they ran the risk that the value of the home could go down.

"When your kids go to college, will the amount that you had been paying on the mortgage be enough to get them through?" I asked. No, they said, they would need to dip into the equity as well. That's why they figured on a line of credit.

"So let's look at what is happening," I said. "You work hard for years to pay off the mortgage early. That money goes into your equity, a place with zero interest, no tax benefit, and a potential for loss but not for gain. And then you turn around and take it out again? What if you lose your job and income? How will you get it out then? The bank won't let you.

"Consider whether it would be a better plan," I said, "to keep your thirty-year mortgage. You have a low interest rate. Pay the minimum, get the bigger tax deduction." I pointed out, however, an important caveat—they must make sure that they save or invest that extra money. The "extra money" is the difference between the fifteen-year and thirty-year mortgage. It could go into a 529 plan, for example, or a Coverdell Education Savings Account, Roth IRA, or life insurance policy's cash value—something with tax advantages.

"If you do that right," I said, "you can win both ways. You can produce tax-free income for college, perhaps get a current tax deduction, and your money will be readily available—and because you haven't paid off the house, you still get the big mortgage interest deduction. All that time, if your house increases in value as you expect, you will be building just as much equity." They wouldn't build up as much equity though through debt reduction, as they are not reducing their debt as fast by making extra payments.

Husband and wife both leaned back in their chairs. They were frowning. "Do you see how you could have the best of both worlds?" I asked.

"No," James said. "We like the other way. We just want to pay off this mortgage and be done with it. We've figured this out—we'll be okay with the school costs."

My job is to lay out the options. My purpose is to help people examine their financial choices in different ways that might work to their advantage. Ultimately, however, the choice lies with the family. Over the next several years, James and Wendy were unable to keep up with the plan to pay off the mortgage before those college expenses hit. Life got in the way, and the money for the extra payments simply was not always there.

The good news is that the children got through college. Unfortunately, their mom and dad ended up wiping out a lot of the equity in their home.

BACK TO THE FUNDAMENTALS

It's a fundamental question, like something out of Finance 101: If you have set aside $1,000 in an investment, and if you also have a $1,000 debt, would it make sense to sell that investment in order to pay off that debt?

Most people can see that doing so would have no immediate effect on their net worth. They are just moving figures from one side of the balance sheet to the other. It's a fairly straightforward balance between what you owe and what you own. Paying the debt means you owe less but you also own less, so the needle doesn't move either way on your net worth.

With that principle in mind, I talk to people about their investments. "How has your portfolio been doing over the years?" I ask. During the last decade or so, they may have responded that the average return has been 6 to 8 percent. "And how about your mortgage rate?" I might hear that it is at 3½ percent. "At those rates," I ask, "would it make sense to use that investment money to pay toward that debt? Would that be a good idea?"

There are many variables. Investments vary dramatically in return and risk, and past performance does not predict future results. Still, most people understand intuitively why paying off a debt that carries a lower interest rate then the investment is earning is not the best move for them. That is what many people are doing, however, when they send extra money to the mortgage company every month instead of putting it into their retirement plan or other investments. They may feel good about paying down that mortgage, but they are sacrificing the potential for investments that could enhance their net worth, in my opinion.

About half of the financial advisors and accountants out there urge people to pay off their homes as soon as possible so that they are free of payments and have more flexibility for retirement. I'm part of the other half who caution their clients to not be in such a rush to do that. If that is your American Dream, and if you will sleep better that way, then I just ask that you explore all of your options.

If you do decide that paying your house off early is the right path for you, then you need to consider just how to do that. You do not need to pay the bank to refinance from a thirty-year to a fifteen-year mortgage. Why not just send in additional payments on your own, avoiding the transaction and management fees? If you do that in a disciplined way, you accomplish similar results without obligating yourself to those additional payments.

Some would say that it's good to obligate yourself because you will be certain to make the payments—because if you do not, you will lose your house. It's easy to say that you will invest that additional $1,000 a month, but if you fail to do so, then you lose that opportunity for gain. Nobody is twisting your arm to set aside that $1,000. Nonetheless, if you twist your own arm, the opportunity is huge. A simple spreadsheet demonstrates. Compare the cost of a mortgage at 3½ or 4 percent interest to the growth of a portfolio at a 6 or 8 percent return. You will see how the portfolio gets to the point where it could pay off the mortgage.

DEBT AMORTIZATION VS. INVESTMENT POTENTIAL GROWTH

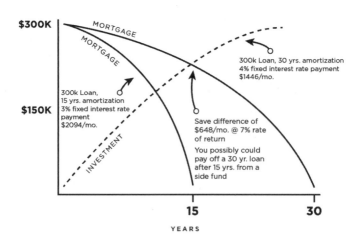

This graph is intended to illustrate a conceptual strategy and is not intended to be interpreted as fact. The hypothetical investment results are for illustrative purposes only and should not be deemed a representation of past or future results. This example does not represent any specific product, nor does it reflect sales charges or other expenses that may be required for some investments.

Every situation is unique, so consider whether a paid-off home is the best thing you could own. It might be among the worst. The millennial generation, for instance, has figured out that home ownership may not be for them, as they are big renters. A house is a major part of the net worth for a great many families—often, the biggest part. It is therefore crucial that it be treated with the appropriate perspective. A family's biggest asset arguably is the ability to produce income and set some of that aside to compound year after year. In time, that power has the potential to build a nest egg greater than the value of the house. Both must be considered in tandem to produce the most beneficial plan for retirement.

I help my clients weigh all of these considerations, and I help to keep them on a disciplined savings and investment plan that they might find more beneficial than simply sinking more money into the equity of their house. I help to hold them accountable to a financial plan with the potential to accomplish their dreams.

CHAPTER 4

THE MASTER OF YOUR FATE

My father grew up in an age when it was expected that companies would take care of their people. You would work for the company three or four decades until you retired. During your working years, along with your salary you received health care, disability income insurance, and other benefits. After your working years, you got a pension—a continuing income for life.

The pension was long the retirement foundation for many families, along with Social Security and whatever else they might have saved. Together, those three income sources were long considered the three-legged stool of retirement planning. It was not until the 1980s, however, in the early days of IRAs and 401(k)s, when my father felt that he had much of an opportunity to save on his own. By then he was well into his working career and already approaching retirement.

Pensions and defined benefit plans in general have been vanishing. Few people today who are planning for retirement have a pension, and they feel that their Social Security benefit is insufficient and unreliable. The responsibility for retirement planning lies heavily on their own backs—and that calls for preparation and education, which many people still are lacking.

Even those who are lucky enough to have a pension might not want to rely on it. Pension plans have been known to go bankrupt, with beneficiaries getting pennies on the dollar of what they had expected for their retirement. A judge's order can liquidate a plan and end a company's responsibility.

It happened to my father after he retired. The company went out of business and declared bankruptcy. The case was in court for years, and his pension plan eventually was basically dissolved. The company's liabilities were waived. Dad ended up getting about half of the pension that he was supposed to receive. I remember those days when I would sit with him and go over the court documents. He had been promised this money as a union member, he said. How could they take it away now? They did.

Most people today have become aware of what can happen. Still, it is not unusual for them to lose track. They might have a pension from an old company but no longer have records of what those benefits should be. Companies get bought and sold and so do the pension liabilities.

I had a client once who had to hire a private detective to determine whether an old pension still existed. It worked. He found the pension. It had been twenty years since he worked at the company, and it had been taken over three or four times. The client had not received any of the pension fund's annual statements in years.

Sometimes that happens because people move and do not notify their former employer where to send those statements—and that's another example of the personal responsibility required in retirement planning today. The longer you let that go, the harder it can be to track down the information. It's important to check every few years. Even if you are years away from collecting on the pension, you need that information as part of your financial planning. Some people may be unaware that they even have one coming to them. Some have found information on unclaimed property websites. Many states have a website for unclaimed assets—I recently helped my mother recover insurance money from that site from when my father passed away. It could be a starting place for people who suspect that they might have overlooked a pension.

PENSION DECISIONS

Once you determine that you do have a pension, then you need to decide which option is best for receiving it. Generally, the retiree can take it as a single life pension at a higher monthly amount or as a joint life pension that pays less monthly but continues the benefit to the surviving spouse at perhaps 50 percent. Even today, I still regularly help people with that decision—particularly teachers and government employees, many of whom still have pensions.

Many people want to provide a 100 percent benefit to the survivor. They feel that it is just the right thing to do. They should stop to think, though, whether the spouse would need 100 percent of the income to support the lifestyle of just one person. The 50 percent survivor benefit might be better. The decision needs to be made in light of expected longevity, the state of each spouse's health, and the retirement income plan in general.

A survivor benefit from a company pension basically is life insurance. When you choose an option leaving something to a survivor, you are buying life insurance. Essentially you are agreeing to accept less money per month up front—in other words, you "pay" more—so that your spouse will continue to have a benefit after you die. What you're doing is buying a pension company's life insurance plan. Instead, you could buy insurance independently. You could choose the higher initial pension payments and then make sure to buy life insurance on your own to provide a lump-sum death benefit to potentially provide a lifelong income for your spouse. This strategy is called *pension maximization*.[3] Considerations for effective implementation of this strategy include but are not limited to the health of the spouses, current and future tax implications, potential rates of return, and the ability of the spouses to handle their own investments or to delegate appropriately.

In recent years, some companies have offered the option of a lump sum payment in lieu of the pension. They are offering that option because they want to get pension liabilities off the books. Just the administration and tracking of all of those accounts gets to be expensive. The lump-sum payout can be an excellent choice—but only if you have a strategy and the discipline to follow it. The responsibility is on you to make sure that money is properly managed for future growth, taxes, and distribution. In a low-interest-rate environment, taking a pension as a lump sum can be particularly favorable for many people. The lower the rate, the larger the lump sum must be to provide the comparable pension amount.

The lump-sum option presents the opportunity to create what amounts to a private pension. Many people are hesitant to take the lump-sum option because they don't want to be responsible for investing it, but their cynical side also tells them that their pension benefits someday might get cut and they could lose them. They don't want to look back with regret. They could use that lump sum to create their own private pension, by investing it in an annuity or other income-producing investments for example. In the case of the annuity, they have their advantages and disadvantages—and there are many types. It would be paid monthly starting at some point in

---

3   Voya Services Company, *Financial Strategies for Successful Retirement* [seminar and workbook], 2017.

the future, just like an employer pension. The difference is that they are working directly with the company that sells the annuity rather than the employer. While they gain a certain amount of control and choice, they also assume an additional level of responsibility. It may or may not be suitable depending on the individual situation.

Many people may choose instead to make use of that lump sum elsewhere, adding it to their portfolio of investments. To avoid taxation in doing so, however, they would initiate a rollover to a qualified plan rather than take a regular distribution. This strategy may appeal to people who already feel comfortable with the amount of guaranteed income that they will be receiving during retirement from Social Security, other pensions, or annuities. However, rollovers from a qualified plan may not be the best decision for everyone, and most employer-sponsored retirement plans have ERISA protections, which may affect the decision. It is important to understand all of your options prior to making a distribution decision. The right approach, of course, will be different for every individual and family.

The pension conversation still is common in our society, although younger people will be increasingly less likely to be facing these decisions unless they are teachers or government employees. For now, pensions remain an important leg of the stool for countless people who already are retired. Our society has seen sweeping changes in how we look at retirement planning, but the security that many people envision themselves with is based on anticipated benefits that are dying fast.

SOCIAL SECURITY

Even as I have been writing this book, the politicians have been continuing to change the Social Security system. Over the years, certain potential advantages for retirees have been stripped away. Most recently, Congress decided to phase out the file-and-suspend strategy for spousal benefits.

The Social Security system is likely not going to disappear. It has become fundamental to the retirement system and the American way of thinking. However, in the years ahead we likely will be seeing more efforts to strip away certain benefits. In its attempts to shore up the system, Congress more than likely will continue to whittle away at Social Security.

A common set of questions is: Should we count on Social Security? Should we make it part of our expectations for retirement income? I tell them that yes, they should make it part of their financial plan. If you are over fifty-five, you have a pretty good chance of getting the majority of the benefit that you were promised. If you are under fifty-five, you may not get everything that you were promised.

You might consider that age to be a rough guideline for where you stand. Financial advisors use different strategies for planning purposes. As for me, when I am working with people who are fifty-five or older, I project that they will be getting somewhere between half of the benefit they had expected and 100 percent of it. For younger families, I project half of the expected benefit.

I would rather err on the side of caution. We can expect to see continuing changes. One possibility is "means testing"—in other words, if the government decides you have sufficient means and enough money, you will not be getting all of your Social Security benefit. Congress certainly could continue to raise the retirement age, as it has done before, and it could tinker in other ways such as trimming survivor and disability benefits. It also might choose to bolster the system by raising the payroll taxation limit above the current cap of income. Both employee and employer could face higher and additional taxes.

In short, I believe that my clients will be getting Social Security, but the benefits may be less than what they originally were promised or what they expected. The system is increasingly depending on fewer workers to support more retirees. That is a big issue. Rather than raise taxes, the government tries to close loopholes and take away ancillary benefits. Certainly there are abuses that should be cleaned up. The politicians have good reason for examining the system to see what might need to be improved. Are demands being made of the system that it was never meant to fulfill? Clearly that is up for debate, but when three ex-wives end up collecting survivor benefits off of one person's benefit—as in the case of longtime late-night host Johnny Carson—then there is legitimate cause to examine the founding principles and consider whether we have gone astray in our expectations.

In previous generations, Social Security amounted to 60 or 70 percent of retirement income. It might be only 30 to 40 percent for the newer generations. Pensions play a much lesser role in today's world, as mentioned earlier. For most people today, the most important leg of the stool will be their personal savings. For many, that means the defined contribution 401(k) plans that have become a central component of retirement planning.

How much should you be putting away for retirement? Many people have long heard that they should be aiming for 10 percent, sometimes called the golden rule of retirement planning. I would certainly like to see that higher, about 15 percent for most people. In general terms, without doing an analysis, I can say that if you are saving that much of your pay in a 401(k)-type plan, and some of it is being matched by your employer, and you also are fully funding a Roth IRA, then conventional wisdom would say you are in a decent position for retirement. Again, everyone's situation differs, and much depends upon retirement age, longevity, and goals.

DECIDING WHEN TO RETIRE

Upon reaching their sixties, one of the first questions on people's minds is the age at which they should retire. Should they do it at sixty-two or seventy or some age in between? Many people want to take their Social Security benefits as early as possible, as soon as they are eligible at age sixty-two. The cynical ones believe that is a good idea simply because they feel that they should grab it while they can, while the system is still intact.

There is much to consider in deciding upon the appropriate retirement age. For one thing, in what kind of health are you and your spouse at this age? How would you assess your likely longevity? In that sense, you might want to claim an early benefit. But there is so much more to consider as well. Every year you can delay receiving a benefit, that benefit will increase by approximately 8 percent before full retirement age. If you retire early, you will face a reduction of benefits.

In working with clients, I review the options to narrow the choices to the ones that will make most sense to them. They might consider a strategy, for example, of delaying their Social Security benefit and living off of their accumulated assets—a 401(k) or Roth IRA or other investments—while the amount of that benefit compounds for a number of years.

When I mention that strategy, people often tell me that it seems contrary to what they had imagined they would do. They had figured that they would be living off of their Social Security benefits while their investments compounded. That's a possibility as well, and it works for a lot of people, but times change and one must consider the current economic environment. In a climate when interest rates are low and market returns are relatively modest, it would be hard to project that investments for the foreseeable future will earn more than 8 percent regularly, the amount that benefits increase annually when retirement is postponed. That needs to be taken into consideration.

As you can see, the Social Security decision should be based on personal circumstances as well as broader economic conditions. These are important matters to discuss with a qualified advisor. Good advice for one family might not be good advice for another. Good advice for last year might not be good advice for this year or for the years ahead. It will depend upon personal savings and investments, income sources and cash flow, health and longevity, even the state of the union and world affairs—a wide variety of factors.

All of it comes down to doing what's right for you—and for a couple, that means both spouses. Sometimes couples treat their retirement concerns as mutually exclusive decisions. A husband may tell me, "My pension and Social Security are mine, and my wife's 401(k) is hers. What she does about her Social Security is up to her, and what I do is up to me."

I see that attitude more often than you might expect, and I try to get couples to see that they should not be making their choices that way and that these are not independent decisions. What one spouse does very likely can have a dramatic impact on the other. For example, let's say the largest income earner lets his or her benefit grow to the maximum at age seventy. When one of the two passes away, the surviving spouse will more than likely continue to receive that higher payment amount.

Therefore, couples must be aware of how individual decisions affect their mutual finances. That principle goes beyond the Social Security decision into all aspects of financial planning. When you are joined together in matrimony, your financial lives are joined as well. It might sound nice to say that each of you is maintaining a sense of independence, but that should not come at the cost of efficient and comprehensive planning that looks out for the best interests of both spouses.

This requires careful oversight. The decision to retire is one of life's big steps, and it must be made with thorough foresight and due diligence. Think of yourself as the CEO of your financial life. I come alongside my clients in a role that they might see as their chief financial officer (CFO). I serve as their source of guidance and accountability.

Retirees today are the masters of their own fate. They must overcome the weaknesses in the Social Security and pension legs of the retirement planning stool. That's a stool with essentially only one good leg remaining, which by definition is no stool at all. It's high time to redefine the analogy. Retirees need to make the most of their own savings and investments. Many people lack the skills and the inclination to manage their own investments, and that is all right—so long as, like any good CEO, they delegate the task to someone who does possess such skills.

CHAPTER 5

THE "RIGHT" ADVICE

Financial setbacks can take the form of either a mistake or a lost opportunity. In his time, my father experienced both. He missed out on a chance for a promising investment when he was young, and later he felt that he was fooled into buying life insurance that he did not need at the time.

The first financial lost opportunity came after the Korean War, when a former army buddy suggested that he invest $1,000 into a stock mutual fund. My father declined, realizing only later that the investment more than likely would have made him a millionaire and put all his children through college. At that time, there were only a handful of mutual funds in existence, so odds were good that any he chose would have blossomed into a fortune in the future.

I recall helping him, when I was a teenager, to fill out the paperwork for a lawsuit against the insurance company. He believed that his agent had persuaded him, unethically, to borrow money from his policy in order to buy a larger and more expensive one. Later in life, my father told me that he felt as if he had been dealing with a used car salesman. The agent did not have his best interests in mind. Dad regretted that he had not been better educated financially and empowered to make wiser decisions. He wished he had a financial advocate on his side. He found out the hard way.

Nobody had ever taught him the financial basics that might have helped him to make better decisions—perhaps to avoid his mistake and to seize his opportunity. They were not taught in the schools, nor in the army, nor in his union shop. They certainly were not taught in the coal regions of Pennsylvania where he grew up. My dad's parents were products of the Great Depression, and the major lesson there was to pinch a penny and live as frugally as possible. My father carried those ways forward into our family, as did my mother, who brought her own life lessons and values.

Most people learn their financial lessons from their parents and those around them as they are growing up, whether family, friends, or neighbors. Early experiences influence them deeply. Often, I will ask clients about those experiences—how they learned about finances, how their parents treated money. By learning about those underpinnings of their attitudes, I can help to lead them to better decisions. I can see whether their views are well shaped or whether they have somehow become distorted. I need to know where to begin with them so that we might make progress. What worked in the past might not be what works best now or into the future.

It is not uncommon, when I ask clients why they own a particular investment, to hear that a friend or family member or even somebody at a party highly recommended it. Does that mean it is the right advice for them? This is one of the financial basics: the "right" investment is the one that is relevant to your situation.

Our attitudes must change with time and circumstances. Once, people traveled by walking, then by horseback, and then buggies and trains and Model Ts and airplanes. We progressed. Likewise, we must progress in our way of thinking, moving beyond the financial lessons of the Great Depression and the war years and developing attitudes and perspectives that will work for us today.

Financial education is improving. Institutions offer financial planning degrees today. Our culture is getting better at this. Still, each of us bears the responsibility to get the very best personal advice, not just something generic that may or may not be applicable.

SOURCES OF BAD ADVICE

Once we have discussed whatever major concern has brought the client through my door, we can move forward to their need for personalized service, for a customized plan, one that will go far beyond generic. Something triggers their realization that they need help, and if they are lucky it happens earlier rather than later.

They also count themselves lucky if they have steered clear of the many questionable sources for financial advice. As my father learned long ago, there are people out there who are eager to talk you into bad decisions. And that advice also can come from friends and family and colleagues and well-meaning people who simply do not know what you need. Or it can come from the media—and you can be sure that none of those commentators knows anything about you.

Questionable advice often originates on the Internet, as well. There are increasingly popular robo-advisors that will try to tell you, based on your income, age, and situation, the investment mixture that is right for you. These recommendations tend to be based on basic demographic info, rather than your complete personal situation.

Sometimes, potential clients will tell me that their 401(k) plan at work includes an investment engine—although they don't use the term *robo-advisor*. "We can just answer a few questions," they say, "and it tells us if we have the right investment mix. It makes suggestions. We can do that for free or for a lower fee than yours—so what is the advantage of working with you?" I explain to them that what they are doing is the equivalent of plugging their symptoms into an online diagnosis program and accepting the results. In a medical scenario, would they make serious health decisions on the basis of that information?

Those simple answers to a few questions reveal nothing about your background. The computer knows nothing about your net worth, your income, your tax bracket, your investment objectives, your time horizon, your risk tolerance, your investment history, or your legacy planning. It doesn't know anything about your situation. It is basing its asset allocation recommendations on your answers to five or ten questions. Nor does the computer know how your spouse's money is invested—and, again, the financial fortunes of spouses overlap and intertwine.

Over and over, it comes back to the same thing—poor advice can result when the source knows nothing about you. The media are giving advice to a mass audience. The people around the water cooler and over the back fence—your friends, neighbors, relatives, colleagues—may know you, but what they care about is their own investments. And they are telling you about their winners but probably not much about their losers. They are at a different stage in life than you. Their situations are entirely different in many respects.

An investment show on television might declare a certain stock a "buy"—but does that mean that you should heed that recommendation? It might be a good buy for you, or it might be a terrible one for you. The media can only offer general information. And if it is a good buy, should it be owned in a qualified or nonqualified account? Should you own it, or should your spouse own it, or should you own it jointly? Maybe it would be best for one of your children. Should you buy it in the name of a trust? How will it affect your tax situation? Are you going to reinvest dividends, or will you be taking them as cash? Will you own it in more than one place with overlap?

For every recommendation, there will be many considerations on the side. Many of the recommendations that you will come across are for growth stocks. Would that make sense for you if you are eighty years old? What could be a strong "buy" for somebody else might be a strong "run" for you.

FINDING A GOOD FIT

A good option is to find a credentialed advisor who holds to a best interest standard. A fiduciary is bound by law—and by integrity—to do only what is in the client's best interest. You will want to be working with an advisor who establishes rapport and trust while tailoring a financial plan with products and services and strategies that help meet your unique needs and goals. A good advisor will provide regular and consistent reviews. You come first. That is the fiduciary requirement. The advice must not merely be suitable for you or for someone like you. It must be best for you as an individual.

It is essential that your advisor be a good fit for you; and I, too, need to determine whether a potential client is a good fit to work with me. In our first meeting, as we talk about goals and dreams, I suggest that together we should be considering four "tests" for our compatibility as client and advisor. Each of us needs to know whether we will have a relationship that will work.

The first is what I call a "chemistry test." Do we think we could work well with each other? Do we have personalities that fit together? This is more or less a general feeling of whether we have a "vibe," a connection.

Second is the "goal test." I am looking to see whether the client's goals are measurable, realistic, and attainable. Would I be able to help to achieve some of those goals? When they seem unrealistic, I may need to tell clients that I might not be the advisor for them and offer to find someone else to work with them.

Next is the "value test." I am looking to see whether I can add value to the clients' current situation and what they are doing. If they already are working with an advisor who is doing a good job and their overall financial situation seems to be in good shape, I simply might not be able to add much value to their financial planning. However, if we each believe that I could add value, and they would want to hear about it, then we probably would be a good fit.

Last is the "asset test." In my years as a financial planner, I have worked with people who are beginners and others who are at an advanced level financially. However, my skill sets and tools and experience work particularly well with the niche of the pre-retiree and the retiree. I look to work with people who are at that stage of life when they have the level of resources and income where my services can be most beneficial to them.

As we conclude our initial discussion, we compare our thoughts on how we feel the conversation has gone. We talk about those four criteria and decide whether we want to continue to the next phase of the relationship. All of that comes before we even dig into the stack of statements that they might have brought with them.

Those are the essentials in determining whether it would make sense for us to work together: Do we have good chemistry together? Could I add value to their situation? Are their goals realistic, achievable, attainable, and measurable? Do they possess that level of resources and income?

In choosing your financial advisor, you will want to look for appropriate credentials as well as the advisor's level of experience and number of clients. What is the advisor's niche market, and do you fit that demographic? What is the advisor's specialty and focus? You can find specific information on advisors at the websites for the Financial Industry Regulatory Authority (FINRA), where you will see a tool called BrokerCheck; at the Securities and Exchange Commission; and at your state insurance commissioner site.

Ask how the advisor is compensated. Is it a fee-based relationship? For example, does the advisor get a flat or tiered fee, hourly fee, or percentage of assets managed? I am typically compensated on a percentage of assets managed. Or does the advisor work on commission for the sale of stocks, bonds, annuities, loaded mutual funds, life insurance, etc.?

From the beginning of my career, I gravitated away from the sales side. I wanted my role as an investment advisor to be a guide and advocate. Yes clients will still need to buy life insurance and to purchase stocks, and I can help them do so—but I recommend that those decisions be made in an advisory capacity, not by a salesperson.

Those who balk at the prospect of paying a fee to an advisor, figuring they can handle it all on their own, should remember this: people do not fail at financial planning because they pay a fee. They fail because things do not get done. They fail because of imprudent decisions. They fail because they follow questionable advice that is inappropriate to their own situation. They do not do the right things, and they make big mistakes and miss big opportunities. Even the talking heads on television and radio usually imply you can't do it on your own and you need their help—you need to watch their shows, subscribe to their newsletters, and buy their DVDs, etc.

The fee that clients pay to an advisor helps them to avoid the pitfalls that trap so many. My father came to understand that, and in my career as a financial educator and advocate I have tried to help many people see the importance of comprehensive financial planning.

"WE'D LIKE TO COME BACK"

Donald and Lucille, with whom I had been working with for quite some time, came in to tell me good-bye. They felt that they should give me an explanation, and this is what they had to say:

> We've enjoyed working with you over the years, and thank you for the great advice. But we were talking with our neighbor. He's not a financial advisor, but he does run a business and he has a lot of experience in finance—and a lot of his investments seem to be doing really well.
>
> So last week we had a cookout at our house, and he asked us why we were paying to work with a financial advisor. "Any time you have questions, just ask me," he told us, "and I'll tell you what you should be doing."
>
> He told us that we should be saving all the money in the fees that we are paying you—and so we figured we would give it a try. We're going to begin working with our neighbor.

I wished them well after explaining why that might not be such a good idea. "I'm still here if you need anything. Maybe I'll check in with you once in a while."

A few years later, we connected again. Lucille said:

> You were right. We were relying on our neighbor, and it was like you said—he wasn't in the same situation as us. He could take risks that we just couldn't handle. He really didn't know what we wanted. He had no idea.
>
> And then it got to be hard just to find a moment to talk with him. We'd see him out mowing the grass, but what

were we going to do, wave him down and start asking about our 401(k)? It never really seemed to work out.

It just wasn't the relationship we thought it would be. We always felt like we were still in the dark when we most needed advice, and it felt like what he had to say just wasn't for us. We'd like to come back, pick up where we left off, and begin working with you again.

We still work together to this day. The couple had gotten a taste of the sort of faulty advice that is so easy to obtain, and they wanted back in a relationship with someone who truly cared about their well-being.

CHAPTER 6

BALANCING THE RISKS

Life entails risks. You cannot make them go away by ignoring them or acting like an ostrich with its head in the sand. To deal with them effectively, you must face them directly. In this chapter, we will examine a variety of threats to the retirement plan and portfolio.

In terms of financial planning, most people equate risk with what can happen to their investments or what might happen to their house or car. In other words, they think of market risk and the need for insurance. They do not necessarily think of such threats as inflation and taxes and fees and interest rate changes, all of which we will review in the pages ahead.

To frame our discussion on risk, it will be helpful to take a look at it from an insurance company's perspective. We can learn much about efficient risk management from the insurance world's view. The risks that can threaten the retirement portfolio go far beyond the kind that can be insured—but let's start with a primer on some insurance fundamentals.

One of the more common questions that I hear from clients involves how to deal with the various risks that they face. Should they be worried or not? Should they deal with the risk, or might they be overreacting? Answering those questions really amounts to properly weighing the situation.

RETAIN, REDUCE, AVOID, TRANSFER

"SUCCESSFUL INVESTING IS ABOUT MANAGING RISK, NOT AVOIDING IT." —BENJAMIN GRAHAM

Any risk can be handled in one of four ways: you can retain it, you can reduce it, you can avoid it, or you can transfer it to someone else. Those choices can be graphed as four quadrants with various combinations of high and low risk and high and low frequency of risk. In other words, how big a blow would you take, and how likely would it be to happen? That can be charted on vertical and horizontal axes.

That's what you will see in the following windowpane chart.[4] It's a chart that can prove useful when making any kind of a risk decision because it clarifies the choices involved. For example, think of the risks of owning a boat. Owning a boat comes with certain inherent risks. You could suffer a loss from damage or abuse or neglect. The chart lays out your choices. You could do nothing and buy no insurance, and that would be retaining the risk. You could take special care of it and learn everything you can about boating, and that would be reducing the risk. You might never use or touch the boat out of fear of what could happen, which would be avoiding the risk. Or you might buy an insurance policy on the boat, thereby transferring the risk.

The intent of insurance is to protect against something that doesn't happen all that often but that would be financially painful if it did. If it happens often, it is a risk that should be reduced or avoided. It tends not to be insurable. What you want to insure are the things that seldom happen but have a great magnitude of loss. If

---

4   Voya Services Company, *Financial Strategies for Successful Retirement* [seminar and workbook], 2017.

the loss would not be so bad, then you would be more likely to retain the risk and see no point in the insurance.

RISK MANAGEMENT BASICS

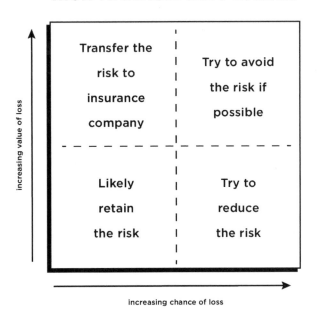

increasing value of loss

Transfer the risk to insurance company

Try to avoid the risk if possible

Likely retain the risk

Try to reduce the risk

increasing chance of loss

I often will suggest that clients consider this graph when they are wondering what they should or should not insure. When they are dealing with something in which the frequency of loss is high—it happens a lot—that typically would be something they might not wish to insure, particularly if the loss would be great, as it would not be cost effective and may not even be insurable.

What are the odds that your house will burn down? Not high. If it happened to you, however, it could be devastating. That is a simple example of the kind of risk that you would wish to transfer. You buy insurance to cover a threat like that. What else do you insure? People insure their homes and cars, and they also insure their lives. If anything happens to them, they want to make sure the family would be all right. The loss would be devastating. They insure against the possibility of becoming disabled. They insure against the potential of needing long-term care, an expense that can deplete the retirement portfolio.

Sometimes they take out insurance when they buy a big-screen television. That's a good example of how a look at the graph can help with the decision. Does the insurance make sense? Is it likely that the TV will stop working? Most people would say that it probably would keep working just fine for years. And the next question is this: If it did break down, would that be a devastating expense? Would it derail their financial plans or disrupt their lives? It's hard to imagine that being the case—and therein lies the answer to the question of whether the TV must be insured, despite the salesperson's prodding. It's an unlikely and minimal risk. That's the kind of risk that people might be better off retaining.

What about risks that happen fairly often but without severe loss? A flat tire, for example—would you insure against that? I know people that have AAA for flat tires but don't believe in life insurance. What about a risk that is likely to happen and would be devastating? Those are the risks that will either be uninsurable or highly expensive to insure, such as the risk of getting injured while skydiving or walking a tightrope.

Those are examples of the various ways to assess risk, which will help in deciding on the appropriate steps to deal with it. The four fundamentals—retain, avoid, reduce, or transfer—can be broadened into many areas of risk management. Those are also the considerations when facing, for example, the risks of unpredictable interest rates, inflation, taxes, fees, medical costs, and early death. A good financial advisor can help you to uncover the range of risks that you will be facing in retirement and determine the best way to handle them. Much is at stake. The potential solutions are many, but they will be based upon those four fundamentals.

First, a quick look at the insurance side: These include property and casualty insurances, for which you can adjust the deductibles to regulate the amount of risk you wish to accept. A high deductible can save a considerable amount in premiums while still protecting against devastating loss. Many people would not report a relatively small claim anyway, for fear of their premiums rising. Certainly your deductible should be at least as high as that threshold that you set for yourself.

Other insurances include disability income and life insurance. Many people identify life insurance as the most important coverage that they could have. Circumstances of course will vary, but for many people under age fifty, disability income insurance can be even more important. Which would be harder on your family, if you were to die, or if you were to become disabled for life and require constant care? In the latter scenario, not only do they lose your income but they gain a major expense.

For the pre-retirees and retirees with whom I work, we definitely focus on the life insurance. Some might ask why it would be important once the nest is empty, but it plays many roles. An early death of a spouse could severely impact the lifestyle of the survivor. In that way, life insurance is more like plan completion insurance. In many families, it also plays an essential role in estate and charitable planning. It is considered one of the best assets to pass on to children because of its generally tax-free status.

"RISK COMES FROM NOT KNOWING WHAT YOU ARE DOING." —WARREN BUFFETT

PROCRASTINATION RISK

Before we take a closer look at the range of risks in retirement planning, I must reemphasize that you must not put off addressing them. Procrastination, for all the reasons that we discussed in chapter 2, is in itself a major risk. It amounts to a decision—the decision not to decide—and I can state categorically that it is a bad one.

How do you deal with that risk, in terms of the windowpane chart? Well, if you continue to procrastinate, you are retaining the risk—and that is hardly a good choice, considering that procrastination is the number-one reason that many people fail financially.[5] You can avoid the risk by taking concerted action. You could reduce the risk of procrastination by agreeing to take one step at a time, addressing issues gradually but at least getting to them eventually. Or you could transfer the risk of procrastination by working closely with a financial advisor who will make sure that important matters get their due attention promptly.

MARKET RISK

Most people are aware of market risk. The confusion lies in the wide variety of opinions as to where the market will be going next and how investors should relate to it.

I worked with Dale a decade ago. He had a large amount of company stock in his 401(k) plan. I discussed with him many times the amount of risk that he was taking with such a concentrated position. We discussed the concept of diversification. I pointed out that he received his salary and many benefits from that company, including health care and a pension plan. In addition, he had a retire-

---

5   Voya Services Company, *Financial Strategies for Successful Retirement* [seminar and workbook], 2017.

ment plan there as well as a substantial amount of stock options. Much of his financial life was related to that one company.

"Your whole livelihood is pretty much based on where you work," I told him. "The one thing they give you where you do have a choice is how you invest your 401(k) money. And yet, looking at your choices there, most of it is in the company. That's where we can do something to spread out your risk."

Dale didn't want to hear it. He was adamant about keeping that large position in the company. The stock options were part of the college planning for his family. He and his wife, Liz, were looking at the 401(k) as their ticket to retirement. I suggested that he consider the Enron scandal, which resulted in that company's stock plunging from over $90 a share in 2000 to less than a dollar the following year. The Enron culture had encouraged investment within the company, resulting in severe losses for many of the employees.

"What could go wrong with my company?" Dale asked. "This is one of the best ones out there. It won't happen to me."

It happened to him. The recession of 2008–09 devastated that family financially. They had to radically change their college savings and retirement plans. The plunge in value of the stock options meant that the children could not afford their first choice of schools. They leaned on loans and scholarships to make it through.

Things were tight all around. The setback definitely compromised the couple's retirement plan. For one thing, they had to dedicate more of their cash flow to the children's college expenses. They lost about half of the 401(k) value—and since they had had their children later in life, this came right at the same time when they were considering retirement.

Their predicament is a prime example of the risk of overconcentration. Some would call it putting too many eggs in one basket. By any name, it is unwise and potentially devastating. It could be the setup for a downfall with reverberations that continue for generations.

It wasn't as if he had not been presented with choices. We had talked about a strategy that would have allowed him to slowly exit the stock options. His concern was that he would be selling at the wrong time, but the concept of dollar cost averaging would have helped to ease that worry. With dollar cost averaging,[6] you gradually purchase shares in a position to spread out the possibility that you might be buying into the investment at a high point. You can use the same concept to average out of positions to spread the risk of selling at a low point—always, of course, keeping tax considerations in mind.

Dale could have been transferring those options slowly into a 529 plan where the money potentially could have grown free of taxes to pay for the college expenses. A 529 plan can have a wide variety of investments, but the parents did not want to go that way. Nor did they wish to diversify among the many choices within his 401(k) plan. And then it was too late. By the time Dale and Liz realized that they were in a sinking ship, there was not much they could do. The stock price eventually recovered, but by that time the children were nearly out of college.

Often, when the market tumbles, you will hear the refrain, "That's okay, it will rebound, don't worry about it." Yes, it probably will—but when? The timing is essential to the good health of the portfolio that is exposed to the market. If you suffer a big loss just as you need to withdraw the money, you might not easily recover.

---

6   Dollar cost averaging does not assure a profit and does not protect against loss in a declining market. Such a plan involves continuous investment in securities regardless of fluctuating price levels of such securities. Investors should consider their financial ability to continue their purchases through periods of falling prices, when the value of their investments may be declining.

It is important, however, to remember the economic and market cycles. Some investors who suffered a big loss in the 2008–09 recession became shell-shocked. They did not get back into the market, and they missed the recovery. That too is a risk. It's the ostrich risk. If you bail out at the bottom, as many did, you might feel that you are hiding in a safe place of cash and money market accounts, but it's riskier than you might think. Not only have you committed the capital sin of selling low, but you are also risking that inflation will erode your savings.

OPPORTUNITY COST

You also are missing out on the chance to put your money to good work. That is the concept of opportunity cost. When you buy a certificate of deposit, the bank doesn't just put your money in a vault to return to you later. It makes use of that money by engaging in investments that will earn the bank more than it pays you. It seizes the opportunity to make money.

When you lose money in the market, you are losing something else—the potential that money would have given you to produce even more. That is your opportunity cost. When you invest for less than you could get, that is an opportunity cost as well. The CD has been called an investment for going broke safely. It is unlikely to outpace inflation in any economic environment. It is like burying money in the backyard. You can dig it all back up someday, but a big part of its purchasing power will be missing.

Think of it this way: if you give a bank $10,000 for a CD, then you in effect have given the bank a loan that it promises to pay back. When you buy a US Treasury bond or savings bond, you are lending money to the government. With a corporate bond, you lend money to a company. In each case, you are promised a stated interest rate and the return of your principal at a certain point. I call those "loanership" investments. They generally don't pay much of a return.

Contrast that to "ownership" investments, which represent something that you possess—such as real estate, stock holdings, or hard assets. They do not always make money, but over the long term they can do very well. That is why when you lend money to the bank—your loanership dollars—the bank often will turn around and invest in something that it can own. It sees the greater potential of the ownership dollars. It converts one to the other for very good reason. Over the long term, the ownership dollars enhance the chance to grow net worth. You do need the loanership dollars for diversification, cash reserves, emergency money, and conservative investments. Typically, however, they will not be the means for building wealth.[7]

OWNERSHIP VS. LOANERSHIP RATES OF RETURN

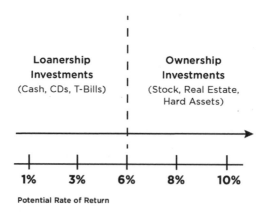

People sometimes ask, "Why should we pay investment fees when the bank is mostly free?" Let me assure you that the bank is

---

7   Voya Services Company, *Financial Strategies for Successful Retirement* [seminar and workbook], 2017.

not free. Banks use your money to make a lot more than you will ever see of it. That's how they pay for the big buildings with the fancy furniture in the lobby. That's how they grow and expand and hire new employees. The service to you is not free—and don't think that they are doing all that with your five-dollar-a-month checking account charge. Similarly, an insurance company doesn't just sit on the money that you hand over for a fixed annuity. It invests that money, creating potential ownership out of the loanership.

As you can see, you run a risk from too conservative a position as well as from too aggressive a position. You are experiencing costs and risks from both, whether you know it or not. When you lose opportunity and expose yourself to inflation's relentless toll, you are facing a threat to your wealth.

I still have clients who look back fondly at the CD rates of the 1980s, when we saw rates in the 13 to 15 percent range. Be careful what you wish for. A return to those rates likely would mean that inflation and taxes would be just as high. That's a climate of high mortgage rates. The pendulum swings. Investors who depended upon CDs or money market rates were in for a rude awakening— and that illustrates the concept of interest rate risk. Ten years ago, investors who felt skittish about the stock market could park in a money market account at 5 percent while waiting for a good time to get back in the market. Recently, such a strategy has meant a return of virtually zero percent. The opportunity cost there is painfully obvious.

VOLATILITY DANGER

Many investors pay close attention to the average annual rate of return that is posted for various securities. The financial industry sometimes points out that stock market returns over the past century have averaged about 10 percent. Yes, that might be the average, but in any given year it can be far to the upside or downside of that. One year it might be up 20 percent, then down 8, up 5, down 30. Many years it might be flat. It's not 10, 10, 10, 10, as many people might think.

The significance of that variation is this: What if you hit that big negative number on the doorstep of your retirement? That is one of the worst things that can happen to you financially at that point. One of the best things to happen would be to have several years of good markets to jumpstart your retirement. Then, if the market turns south, you will have built up your resources to handle it.

As you can see, the sequence of returns matters more than the average annual rate in the performance of your individual portfolio. Market downturns come regularly, and your financial plan must encompass more than trying to beat the market. If the S&P 500 index loses 30 percent and your portfolio is down only 25 percent, you are still not going to be cheering.

In many cases, your portfolio must be built with sufficient diversity to withstand the volatility of the market. Some investors can tolerate larger fluctuations of gains and losses than others, so you and your advisor need to decide on an asset allocation strategy that meets your needs and goals. Then you should rebalance that allocation annually to make sure those percentages do not change—as tends to happen as winning positions outpace losing ones.

LONG-TERM-CARE RISK

This is another of the risks that people are not so eager to talk about. Along with becoming disabled and dying, going into a nursing home is not a fun prospect to anticipate. Nonetheless, this is a very real risk that can be financially devastating. It must be addressed.

Years ago, long-term-care insurance did not exist. People did not imagine themselves living for the long term, and so it simply was not a worry. The grandparents or the great-grandparents, if they needed care, could live with one of the children. The extended family was closer. Society has changed, and those children might live on an opposite coast or be so tied down with their own obligations that they cannot look after the prior generation. As a result, long-term care has become a hot-button issue.

As people live increasingly longer, their bodies begin, inevitably, to slow down. And yet improvements in medical care at the same time can keep people alive for decades, even in a frail state. Whether that is good or bad, it certainly is costly. To pay for the cost of care, families may need to sacrifice their life savings—unless they plan well in advance for that possibility. In surveys, respondents of retirement age often say that they are more afraid of running out of money than they are of dying.

I suggest that every client should have a long-term-care plan. For some, the plan amounts to doing nothing. In other words, they choose to self-insure—and if they have the resources and have thoroughly discussed the matter, that may be all right. Generally, however, this would be an option that only people with a net worth of multiple millions should be considering. Even then, it would make sense to use insurance dollars to leverage the amount of money available to protect against such a loss. As we have seen, when an event could be financially devastating but may have a low chance of happening, it makes sense to transfer the risk to an insurance company. That way, an affluent family might be paying a relatively minimal amount in order to be sure that they will have a much larger bequest for their children.

Those who choose not to self-insure have a number of options. One is traditional long-term-care insurance. You purchase a policy that covers you in the event that you need the care. If you die without needing that care, you get no benefit for the premiums that you have paid for all those years. Many people find that to be a terrible waste of money. Why pay for something you do not use? They might wish to consider whether they would be upset if they didn't wreck their car despite paying for automobile insurance. Would they be upset if their house never burned down despite the premiums that they pay?

Regardless, from a pragmatic standpoint, most people do not like the idea that they are spending money on long-term-care premiums that they might never get back. What has become more popular in recent years is a hybrid solution where people either use annuities that have long-term-care riders, or they use life insurance with an accelerated benefit rider or a critical care rider. Often they use some combination of life insurance and long-term-care insurance.

Whichever approach you take, talk it through with your family. You should discuss and agree upon a strategy, and it should be an integral part of the financial plan for retirement, whether it is self-funding, traditional long-term care, or a hybrid solution. The right choice will be different for every family. Long-term-care and longevity risk is increasingly acute in our society, and it simply cannot be ignored.

A capable financial advisor can help you determine if the insurance is affordable. For many, it is—but not for all. I have advised some couples that in their particular situation they cannot afford to cover that risk and that they instead should rely on family and existing assets.

Some people are looking for a way to get some of the money back that they spend on premiums, and there are policies that do offer return-of-premium features—but that comes at a cost. Insurance in my opinion wasn't meant for such bells and whistles. It was meant to protect against the big loss.

In a way, the long-term-care risk illustrates a fundamental risk that seems to be at the root of many of the others—and that is the potential of simply living a long time. To live a good long life is hardly something that should be called a risk (maybe it should be called a bonus), but it does come with financial obligations. The goal of retirement planning is to preserve the accustomed lifestyle for many years to come.

CHAPTER 7

THE THREATS WITHIN

"FOCUS ON WHERE YOU WANT TO GO, NOT ON WHAT YOU FEAR." —ANTHONY ROBBINS

Sam and Caroline had radically different views regarding their finances. I had been working with the couple for about a decade, and they were now in their fifties. She was highly conservative, almost to the point of paranoia, and seemed terribly intense when she talked about world affairs and the economy. By contrast, he welcomed the excitement of the markets and could accept risk and volatility in exchange for growth opportunity. He handled their investments, and he was in it for the long term, always looking for the end goal down the line.

For Sam, however, there wasn't going to be a long term. Cancer took his life. Afterward, as I met with Caroline in several meetings, I encouraged her to focus now on her own situation. She was only in her early fifties and could live another four decades. However, she invariably turned the discussion to a world of woe. She spoke of ISIS and terrorist attacks. She foresaw a nuclear nightmare in North Korea and the Middle East. She bemoaned the collapse of oil prices, the insanity of the presidential elections, and the Zika virus. She worried about all those matters and a dozen others.

I tried to get Caroline to see that none of those issues needed to alter her long-term vision of retirement. I told her that if she could read the *Time* magazine articles and newspaper headlines from generations past, she would undoubtedly see these words: "stock market collapse" and "energy shortage" and "terrorist attacks." She would read about famine and disease and pestilence. I pointed this out not to deepen her despair but rather to offer her a sense of perspective. Today's issues and tragedies are echoes of a theme. The news repeats itself. Through it all, life goes on—and so does the market.

Still, she couldn't get past it all. She wanted to bury her head in the sand. That was her solution. She transferred all of her assets into CDs, for a return of less than 1 percent, and soon she totally cut off her advisory relationship with me. This was her way of getting away from the stress.

Life doesn't work that way. We cannot flee, and we cannot hide. We each contribute in our own way to the world as we know it, and we must do our best to leave it better than where we found it. In doing so, however, we must overcome more than the external risks of market and inflation and all the other forces that threaten to wreck the retirement portfolio. Perhaps the greatest risks lie within the human heart and the human brain.

With our inherent biases and behaviors, we can be our own worst enemy. In this chapter, we'll take a look at some of the attitudes and tendencies that can lead people to less-than-ideal decisions. These have everything to do with financial and retirement success, but they seldom are included in textbooks or taught in classes.

What are your fundamental beliefs about money? What were you taught as a child about its role in society and in your family? Do you and your spouse see eye to eye on money matters? Which political views on economic issues do you embrace? All of those questions get to the heart of behavioral finance. Your attitudes and beliefs will inform your decisions, which will influence the course of your life. That is why you need to be aware of these powerful predispositions.

FEAR, HOPE, AND GREED

> "IF YOU CANNOT CONTROL YOUR EMOTIONS, YOU CANNOT CONTROL YOUR MONEY." —**WARREN BUFFET**

The cycle of fear, hope, and greed is not only the basis for the ups and downs of a personal portfolio but it can also explain the great economic cycles of expansion and contraction. This is a reflection of human behavior.

As the market rises, so too do the spirits of investors. They feel optimistic and excited. They are thrilled by the return they are making and the prospect of more to come. This is the atmosphere where greed can set in. They are riding a roller coaster to a peak of euphoria. Higher and higher, more and more—they want to buy an ever larger dose of what is making them feel good, almost like a drug.

Everyone around them seems to be doing the same. This is the phenomenon known as the herd mentality. Investors run with the bull when everyone else is doing so, and they run away from the bear when that seems to be the prevailing pattern. That's what causes rallies and selloffs that do not seem to make sense considering the economic conditions.

It happens with the market in general, and it happens with every asset class. We have seen bubbles in technology stocks, real estate, high-yield bonds, oil, and others. Investors are riding high—until, at the peak of the frenzy, the binge is over. Down comes the coaster. Greed yields to anxiety and fear, even to despondency. It's a scary ride to the bottom, but then hope builds anew and the investors look for signs that maybe it wasn't all that bad. They find those signs, and they start the climb, at first slowly as optimism builds, then faster as greed renews its grip. In time, it's back to fear and hope.[8]

HUMAN BEHAVIOR AND THE ECONOMIC CYCLE

As Sir John Templeton, the noted philanthropist and mutual fund pioneer, observed, **"Bull markets are born on pessimism, grown on skepticism, mature on optimism, and die on euphoria."**

A sense of unbridled excitement is what can lay investors low, according to investment guru Warren Buffett. "If they insist on trying to time their participation in equities," he explained, "they should try to be fearful when others are greedy and greedy when others are fearful."

---

8   Voya Services Company, *Financial Strategies for Successful Retirement* [seminar and workbook], 2017.

Unfortunately, they follow the crowd. That is not the way to make money, nor is buying high and selling low—but that's what people do when they are caught in that cycle and fail to understand their own behavior.

Here's an overview of several other investor biases that can wreak havoc on a portfolio:

Home country bias. Investors tend to want to focus their money on the domestic market, as in: "I'll only invest in American companies." They are more familiar with the companies that do business within their borders. They tend to view domestic securities more favorably and optimistically than they look at the foreign markets. They therefore may not diversify into international holdings, and their failure to do so could weaken their portfolio if the domestic economy falters. What they may not realize is that many of those American companies generate much of their profits overseas, through subsidiaries or international production facilities. Many people, given a list of well-known companies, would have a hard time distinguishing which ones are foreign owned. We live in a global community, and to exclude international markets can be shortsighted.

Recency bias. Investors tend to base decisions on the belief that what they recently have experienced will keep happening. They behave like the gambler who sees the roulette ball land on red for five spins in a row and falsely concludes that the odds favor red for the sixth spin. The market crashes, and investors keep their distance, expecting that it will crash again. The market rallies, and they invest as if they have never seen a downturn. That bias tends to lead people to buy high and to sell low and to fail to invest in a way that takes advantage of natural cycles.

Information overload. The more choices, the better the decision, people believe. What happens, however, is that they may become paralyzed by uncertainty. We are bombarded with information every hour of every day over our laptops and smartphones and through the social media, not to mention the old media of broadcast and print. Faced with so many choices, many people end up doing nothing, suffering not only market losses but also opportunity costs. A 401(k) retirement plan may not be serving the best interest of participants when it has too many choices on the investment menu, as participants may feel their choices are overwhelming which can lead to indifference.

Confirmation bias. When they strongly believe something, people go looking for information to confirm it. They ignore whatever doesn't fit. First, they form their conclusion, and then they look for the opinions and the facts that seem to back it up. Such predispositions easily can lead investors astray. They read an unfavorable news account and bail out of a stock, ignoring reports of exciting developments at the company. They miss the upswing when those developments pay off.

Loss aversion. People tend to fear loss much more intensely than they desire gain. That tendency leads them to favor the status quo and prevents them from taking action. They would rather make no decision than risk a bad one. They feel reluctant to try a different approach because if it doesn't work out for them, they would feel worse than if they had done nothing at all. Investors may strongly suspect that they should trade an investment, but the prospect that it would be the wrong choice—and that it might hurt them—stops them in their tracks. Like the woman in the opening story of this chapter, they and their portfolios succumb to pessimism.

Portfolio meddling. Your overall rate of return can suffer if you make too many frequent changes to your portfolio. It is, of course, wise to take a tactical approach based on good information, but often these changes do not fit that description. Because of the aforementioned cycle of "Fear, Hope, and Greed" it is possible that the more often investors tinker with their portfolios, the less return they may get over the long run. I have worked with clients who call me monthly, wanting to constantly alter their mix based on whatever they have heard in the news. Other clients agree to a strategy and want me to rebalance as necessary. They seldom change anything. Those in the second group typically do better with their investments.

The Ellsberg paradox. This particular bias was popularized by Daniel Ellsberg, renowned for releasing the top-secret Pentagon Papers on US decision making during the Vietnam War. In essence, it refers to people's tendency to avoid uncertainty and ambiguity. We shy away from the unknown. In one study, participants were asked to choose a red ball out of one of two bags. They were told that one bag had fifty red balls and fifty black balls. The other bag had an unknown mix—for all the participants knew, it might have contained only red balls. Most of the participants chose the known entity. They reached into the bag with a fifty–fifty mix. They were more comfortable knowing the odds than risking the unknown.

Framing. This is the human tendency to make decisions based on how something is presented to us. If we are told that a surgical procedure has a 95 percent rate of survival, then it will seem to be a safer choice than if we are told that the same surgery has a 5 percent probability of causing death. If we read on a label that a food is 95 percent fat-free, does that not sound like a better choice than if we were to read that it contains 5 percent fat?

Hindsight bias. Hindsight, they say, is 20/20. This bias refers to the illusion that the events of the past were more predictable than they actually were. Observers may believe that they clearly see a cause and effect, but the reality is likely much more complex. It all seems clear in hindsight—but at the time, the choices probably were not so simple. In hindsight, investors and analysts and media pundits look at financial bubbles and point out how everyone should have seen the indicators that they were about to burst. It was so obvious, they say—but if that were the case, it is unlikely that the bubble would have grown. Investors who are inclined to hindsight also may feel overly confident that they can predict future results based on their gut feelings rather than on analysis. Wise investors understand that crystal balls are in short supply.

PIGGY BANK LESSONS

In working with many people over the years, I sometimes have tried to help them see how one or another of these behavioral finance issues might be influencing their decision-making. Our attitudes toward money are shaped in many ways, and often the roots are in childhood. They are less likely to do us harm when they are out in the open where we can acknowledge and understand them.

My focus on financial education and advocacy has mostly been oriented toward adults, although I have gone into schools to teach teenagers the basics, including how to open a checking and savings account. I also have emphasized to parents the importance of teaching the fundamentals of money management to their children beginning at an early age. That is when they can make a deep and lasting impression on the power of saving, the importance of setting goals, and the enduring value of giving back a portion of what has been given to us.

Parents often debate whether giving children an allowance is a good idea or whether they should be obliged to work for their pay. Either way, I believe that what is important is how they deal with that money. Is there any further supervision and direction? I suggest three separate piggy banks. For every dollar they receive, eighty cents will go into the first piggy bank, to be used for some big, long-term goal or desire—not necessarily saving for college but perhaps buying a bike. The second piggy bank is for use any time or for emergency money. For each dollar, a dime goes in there. The third bank is for charity, which gets that final dime, the 10 percent share that you might call tithing or you might call giving back or paying it forward.

PIGGY BANK LESSONS FOR CHILDREN

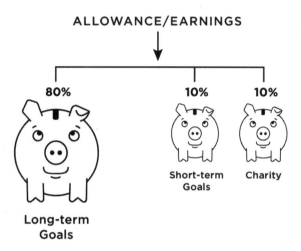

That's a powerful way to teach values and the underpinnings of money management. It teaches small children how to postpone immediate gratification in favor of a greater cause. Many people, of course, will come by those skills naturally in time, but as you already have seen, "the earlier the better" is a prevailing theme of this book. Time is a powerful driver when it is harnessed early in life.

This is not the way that I learned about money when I was a child. Few children get that lesson from their parents or grand-parents. The schools today are getting somewhat better at teaching financial basics, but they have a long way to go. I graduated from Penn State with a business degree, and I took courses in economics, marketing, finance, and accounting. I never took a single course on financial planning. It wasn't offered.

There are many young people out there launching their careers who still have not mastered the piggy banks. Some haven't figured it out even when it's time to retire. Yes, an adult's concerns are somewhat different than that of a five-year-old or a ten-year-old, generally. Still, the principles do not change. Those piggy banks are pretty much the same, even though they bear the fancy names of various vehicles for asset allocation and investment.

Financial savvy comes down to some basic sets of rules, just as there are rules for football and baseball and soccer. We introduce the rules of sports to children when they are little because that is when they take to them most naturally. Little kids quickly learn to balance on skis, or ice skates, or a bike—and they have less distance to fall. That is when they can best learn the basics, and that is when they can best stand back up and dust off their knees. You're not swinging at a T-ball at age twenty-three, I hope. You did that in kindergarten. Nor should you wait so long to learn about money.

Experience has been the primary instructor for most of us. As things go wrong or go right, we learn. That is the way it was for the young version of me and for many of those whom I've met. So many of us find out along the way what is important, and we develop the attitudes and behaviors that work for us—or, too often, that don't work. This is the essence of what I have learned and what I wish to tell others: money matters because people matter. Everything else must be built upon that.

CHAPTER 8

BE TAX WISE

Henry and Nora had accumulated significant wealth and were looking forward to tapping into it as they began the pursuit of their retirement dreams. There was a roadblock on their path, however, and it was called taxation.

Most of their accounts were in pretax dollars, and they could not touch that money without paying the long-postponed tax. As a result of a lifetime of saving money in their 401(k)s and IRAs, the couple had tucked away 95 percent of their net worth into tax-deferred accounts, not necessarily on my watch. In working with them on their distribution planning, I explained how much would need to be allocated toward those taxes.

"Whoa!" they said. "We don't want to be paying that much in tax!" I explained that under the circumstances, they had limited choice. They told me that they did indeed have a choice they preferred—and that would be to live more frugally and cut back on their lifestyle, anything to avoid that tax hit. They said that they just couldn't bear having to pay that much. They decided to live on less.

In doing so, Henry and Nora were creating another snowball. They were putting themselves in the position of leaving to their heirs what is potentially a troublesome asset from a tax perspective, which is a 401(k) or an IRA with pretax dollars. If the heirs receive that money as a taxable lump sum, which is often the case, much of it vanishes immediately to the IRS. If Henry and Nora had been working with me during their accumulation years, we could have done much to alleviate that situation. As it stood, their choices were still limited. All of their lives they had been urged to save their money pretax, to put it in the 401(k) and the IRA—and when they got to retirement, the tax party was over. They had built up a lot of wealth that they were reluctant to use.

I have seen that situation with many couples. The attitude seems to be that they do not need a financial plan and that they will be in good shape for retirement as long as they stick as much money as possible into their 401(k). Then comes the surprise.

EXPENSIVE MISTAKES

There's an old saying in the industry that you should not let the tax tail wag the investment dog, meaning that you should not make your investment decisions based solely upon the tax situation. However, people work hard for their money. They work for years to advance their careers and get those raises and bonuses, sometimes working a second job. If they let a lot of money fly out the window by paying unnecessary taxes, what was the point of all that hard work on the front end? They need to protect the money on the back end.

I often have seen cases where people have made mistakes or missed opportunities to save on taxes. I have seen people struggle to pay off their mortgages early—and mostly what they are doing is stripping away their ability to use the biggest tax deduction possible. I have seen people exercise their stock options incorrectly, ending up paying ordinary income tax versus potentially paying long-term capital gains rates.

THE LEAKY
NET WORTH BUCKET

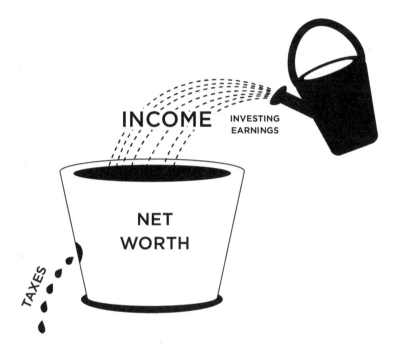

Although not a prevalent situation for everyone, I have seen situations where people might have saved tens of thousands of dollars if only they had been aware of a little-known provision of federal tax law called the NUA (net unrealized appreciation) rule, which allows favorable tax treatment of certain distributions of company stock from a 401(k) plan, and may be beneficial when the stock has greatly appreciated. At the time of distribution, only the cost basis of the shares—the amount originally paid for them—is subject to tax. The remainder, or NUA, is not taxed until the stock is sold and then at the favorable capital gains rate. This sometimes presents the opportunity to position

401(k) money better for tax purposes—but it is not a strategy you are likely to read about in *Money* magazine as it is not a common occurrence and therefore probably won't sell too many copies. It can also be dangerous having too much company stock in the 401(k), as in the Enron example mentioned previously.

Those are just a few examples of big tax mistakes that can be costly to the retirement portfolio. Most people, however, do not suffer a major blow. They suffer from leaks, year after year. Benjamin Franklin wisely cautioned, "Beware of little expenses. A small leak will sink a great ship." If you think of your net worth as one big bucket, there are only two ways to fill it and keep it full: either put more stuff into it, or plug the leaks. One of those leaks is taxation, and you need a fix that will last.

CPAs tend to focus on getting an immediate refund and tax savings for their clients but not necessarily about the tax situation in a decade or two or during retirement. Over the years, I have had friendly disagreements with CPAs as to whether a client should consider IRA or Roth IRA contributions, when they should exercise stock options, and how they should distribute their investments among tax-free, tax-deferred, and taxable accounts. Time and again I have seen that the CPA's perspective is what is in it for the client today with the current tax return, which I can appreciate. However, as a financial advisor that does not provide specific legal or tax advice I help my clients take a long-term view that goes beyond today's savings for a bigger benefit later. I have found that many people are unaware of the wide variety of ways in which they can use the tax laws to their advantage.

THREE TAX BUCKETS

Many people find it easier to think visually about how their money is being used and distributed. It can help to mentally separate the money by the goals for which it is intended. They like to know that a particular asset has been set aside for a particular use.

One such means of mental accounting is to think of three tax buckets containing three categories of assets—taxable, tax-deferred, and tax-free. Many people focus on the rate of return and whether they should have US or foreign investments, large-cap or small—but they do not think as much as they should about how the gains on those investments will be taxed. As an investment strategy, they do not take tax diversification into consideration.[9]

3 TAX BUCKETS

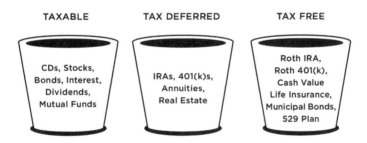

TAXABLE	TAX DEFERRED	TAX FREE
CDs, Stocks, Bonds, Interest, Dividends, Mutual Funds	IRAs, 401(k)s, Annuities, Real Estate	Roth IRA, Roth 401(k), Cash Value Life Insurance, Municipal Bonds, 529 Plan

We do not know what will be happening to tax brackets in the future, neither can we be certain about how the tax rules might change. We can only base our planning on what we know now and perhaps look back in history for the patterns that might offer us guidance.

---

9   Voya Services Company, *Financial Strategies for Successful Retirement* [seminar and workbook], 2017.

Let's take a look at each of those three buckets of tax diversity and see what we might find in each of them.

Taxable bucket. Many people feel that they should avoid this bucket simply because it doesn't sound as advantageous as the other two. "Why would I want to have assets in a taxable bucket?" you might ask. It's a good question. In general, certainly you do want to avoid paying unnecessary taxes. However, there are reasons that you would consider using the taxable bucket. In it you would put such investments as stocks and bonds, mutual funds, and CDs—investments that are taxable in the year in which they realize a gain. Losses could be realized or unrealized as well.

The number-one reason to use the taxable bucket is liquidity. If you are saving in a tax-deferred or a tax-free account, there is a good chance that you have limited access to that money. If you need it, there may be a penalty to access it. Before the 2008–09 recession, it was more common for clients to talk about retiring as early as possible, potentially in their fifties. Many tax-deferred and tax-free accounts cannot be accessed until age 59½. Having a taxable pool of money allows you in general to access that money before the typical retirement age.

It also usually gives you the most flexibility. You can use those funds for whatever reason you choose—for college, to help the children or grandchildren, for an early retirement, for a major purchase. For a variety of reasons, you may not be able to tap into your retirement account for those expenses.

Tax-deferred bucket. This one tends to be the biggest for most people because it represents their 401(k)s or IRAs and tax-deferred annuities. That might sound like a good deal. After all, the taxes are being deferred until later. You're not paying taxes on the growth of the account now, and you may get a tax deduction or tax-favorable treatment for those dollars when you put them into the account. As a result, you are able to put even more money into it. Because of the tax deduction, it might actually cost you only $70 to put $100 into a 401(k) account, depending upon your tax bracket.

The good news is that you can save a lot of taxes up front. Your money grows tax-deferred and the account snowballs during your working career and can become quite substantial by retirement. When it is time to start taking distributions, taxes are due on those contributions and earnings. You may or may not be in a lower tax bracket at that time. People love to see the large balance in their 401(k) plan and their IRA, and they love those tax deductions and tax savings up front—but upon retirement, the reality kicks in. At age seventy and a half, they are usually required to begin taking annual distributions and paying taxes on the money.

It's a quite useful bucket for tax diversification. It can be used to great advantage—but in my opinion the bucket should not become so large that it overwhelms the size of the other two buckets. You want to keep your options open as to which bucket will make the most sense for you to use.

The tax-free bucket. The advantage of using the tax-free bucket is pretty obvious—any money that you take out of it is free of taxation. If you ask people randomly which of the three buckets they would prefer, this is the one they choose. But it is also typically the bucket in which they have the least amount of money. It would stand to reason that they should be using this bucket more. Tax-free assets may include municipal bonds, life insurance, Roth IRAs, and 529 plans.

Certainly one of the downsides to using the tax-free bucket is that you have to pay tax on the front end. You're using post-tax dollars to put money into this bucket, but in doing so you may be allowing it to grow tax-free. There may be some limitations on your liquidity for vehicles in this bucket, however, once again your individual situation has much to do with the decision. You have to think about what your tax bracket is going to be at retirement. You have to think about what is going to happen to income tax rates in the future.

WHICH BUCKET TO CHOOSE?

Different people need different tax buckets at different times. For someone in a lower tax bracket, for example, the tax-free equivalent yield of a municipal bond might not make sense. And a 529 plan might have tremendous legacy planning and estate planning features in it, but it may not be the right choice if you have no children or grandchildren.

So much depends upon the individual—those goals and dreams, lifestyle, risk tolerance, investment history and objectives, time horizon. You cannot just wave a wand and decide how much will go into each bucket and which bucket should be used first for withdrawals. I can state some generalities that will influence the decision:

- The tax-free bucket is a logical option to pass to future generations, for the most part. As people live ever longer, that money has a chance to compound dramatically. Since it may be the last bucket they ever access, it is a likely one to go to their heirs.

- The tax-deferred bucket may not be a good option to leave to children, since they will have to pay the taxes when they receive those assets. Since this is the biggest bucket for most people, it makes sense to start using it in retirement. Many times the children are in higher tax brackets than the parents. They might be able to stretch the distribution of the inheritance over their lifetimes, but still they will owe plenty to the government. Once you add up the federal, state, and local taxes and the potential estate and inheritance taxes, they could lose half of the account value or more by the time they get the money. There are other strategies to move some of this money to the tax-free bucket that can be explored as well.

- You will not necessarily be in a lower tax bracket when you retire. Most retirees expect to continue receiving a sizable income. They expect to take vacations and to enjoy life and to spend money with their kids and grandkids. That requires taking income from assets. Today's tax rate is at a historical low. The top federal income tax rate for an individual is 39.6 percent. In the 1970s, it was 70 percent, and during the 1940s and 1950s, it was over 90 percent.

Might such rates return? We have a Social Security and Medicare system in trouble and a government with $17 trillion in debt. Who's going to pay? Probably the taxpayers. History would indicate an upward trend.

HIGHEST MARGINAL TAX RATE, 1913-2014

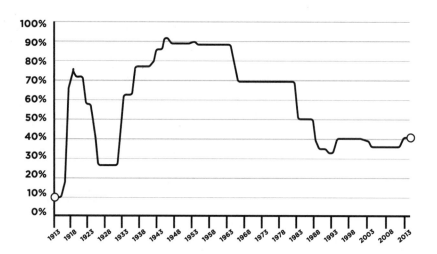

Source: Tax rates shown are from the Tax Foundation.

http://www.taxfoundation.org

- If you will not be spending your required withdrawals from a 401(k) or traditional IRA, consider what to do with that money. I have met people who just withdraw the money, pay the hefty tax, and stick it into a bank account at a low rate, paying tax again on that interest. Not only are they being taxed twice, but they are losing a lot in opportunity cost as that money languishes there. By contrast, a Roth IRA has no required minimum withdrawal, and no taxes are due whether it is you or your heirs who eventually take the money out, provided it is considered a "qualified" withdrawal by the IRS.

USING A 401(K) WISELY

As pensions have been fading away in our society, the 401(k) and similar plans have become the primary means by which most people are preparing for retirement. And they will need to use this tax bucket to their best advantage or they could be in for some unpleasant surprises. Overall, however, these plans are a huge benefit for a great many people. They can make saving for retirement a fairly easy and painless process through payroll deductions.

The old way of saving for retirement was more or less the cookie-jar approach—if anything was left over at the end of the month, you would set it aside in your savings. For many people, that doesn't work. Nothing ever seems to be left over—and so month after month, nothing gets saved. Nothing compounds. What works better is the concept of "pay yourself first." The money for retirement comes out before you pay your bills.

By contrast, you never see those pretax dollars before they go into your 401(k). Somehow at the end of the month you have still found a way to pay your bills. It's as if the money for the 401(k) was never there—but you can rest assured that it is there, and if properly managed it can work hard for you.

The practice of gradually and continually contributing to these retirement plans offers significant advantages. The problem with lump-sum investing is that many people never get a lump sum to invest. What they do have is a bit of their paycheck that they can put away regularly, every week or every month which then has the potential to compound and grow. Investing that way actually serves them quite well. It helps them to take advantage of fluctuations in the market and the prices of securities. If the price of an investment goes down, they get to buy it at a lower price, reaping the reward later when it hopefully rises. Remember the earlier discussion about dollar cost averaging? By purchasing in increments, they can avoid the danger of dumping a lot of money into an investment when it is at an all-time market high—and then having the rug pulled out from under it. That is another example of how dollar cost averaging can go far toward helping reduce investment risk.

It also is a discipline that helps investors to abide by the time-tested rule that the way to make money is to buy at a bargain. A young acquaintance once showed me his 401(k) statement. "Look here, it's up 20 percent just in the last year!" he beamed.

"Oh that's too bad," I responded. "I'm really sorry that happened to you."

"Huh?"

"Yeah, I'd rather you have shown me that you lost money in your 401(k) last year." He looked at me incredulously. I continued: "You are contributing to it every week. So do you plan to retire within the next ten years?"

"No, but . . ."

"Then theoretically what you want for now is to see those investments going down in value. That way you can buy more of them with your dollars and own more shares. The more shares you own, the better off you will be when they gain ground years from now. It's when you are getting ready to retire that you want to see those big gains—not now."

I have challenged people a number of times that way, and they generally respond with furrowed brows. But they do see my point. It is not always as important to see your 401(k) grow in value when you are younger and putting money into it. That's the time to be taking advantage of the opportunity to buy at a lower share price.

In years past, many people were concerned that their 401(k) money was not liquid, basically unavailable until retirement, and in the meantime the company controlled the money, with limited investment choices. Many of those concerns have waned, and people's faith in the 401(k) has grown.

Nonetheless, I still see people leaving a lot of money on the table when they fail to take advantage of another huge benefit: the company match. That's essentially free money. Let's say your company matches fifty cents on every dollar that you put in, up to your contribution limit. If you are contributing 6 percent of your pay, that means that the company is giving you another 3 percent. How do you turn that down? Even if you were to withdraw the money the next year and pay the taxes and penalty, you would still be ahead of the game because of that company match.

Don't get me wrong: I am not at all recommending that you withdraw your money early. You would be robbing yourself of the compounding power over the years. However, do not underestimate the value of that company match. It is a valuable benefit. In addition, it is important that you spread out your contribution over the entire year. Many companies match on a quarterly basis, and if you skip a quarter you could miss out. You also are missing out on the dollar cost averaging advantage.

In general, you should at least put into the plan the amount that the company will match. If you have the ability to save more than that for retirement, you will want to be looking at a Roth IRA or a Roth 401(k). Beyond that, you might then contribute more to the pretax 401(k) and then consider other tax-free or tax-deferred investment opportunities.

THE ROTH ALTERNATIVE

If you asked me where people were missing out the most on potential tax advantages, I would point to the Roth IRA. I believe that it is a financial sin to not use the Roth to your advantage. Whether you are contributing to one or finding a way to convert to one, you will do well if you own investments in this major tax-free vehicle for retirement saving.

The Roth IRA is the namesake and legacy of its chief legislative sponsor, Sen. William Roth of Delaware, and it was inaugurated as part of the Taxpayer Relief Act of 1997. The government does not provide many opportunities to save tax-free for the rest of your life and to put almost anything you want as an investment vehicle into that tax-free account. For that reason, it is important to understand how you can make best use of this opportunity. Some wonder if it is too good to be true—will the government change the rules and strip away the power of the Roth? It might. But those who already have one likely would be grandfathered. That is the approach the government typically takes. As it stands, the Roth IRA simply is too good an opportunity to ignore.

How does one know whether the Roth IRA is the best choice? My answer once again reflects a truth about so many other elements of comprehensive financial planning: it depends upon your situation. What is your tax bracket? What is your life expectancy? What are your intentions for estate planning? I cannot give you a blanket answer, other than to say that the Roth IRA has many applications and it is likely that you will find some benefit to you.

It can make sense, as well, to convert your traditional IRA or 401(k) money into a Roth. Over the years I have helped clients do just that, after talking through the virtues and the downsides including possible liquidity limitations. Some but not all CPAs tend to frown on the concept of a conversion. They are thinking about the current tax ramifications—when you convert, you have to immediately pay the taxes that have been deferred. But they are not thinking so much about the future advantages—the Roth can produce a supply of tax-free money in retirement that will enhance income without jacking up the tax bracket.

Here are some of the questions that can determine whether a conversion would be a favorable strategy:

- Is your tax bracket currently average or below average? Are you at least ten years away from retirement, and do you expect to be in the same tax bracket or a higher one when you retire?

- What is your expectation on the future direction of tax rates? Do you believe that they will be rising? How much money do you currently have available in a tax-free bucket? Would it benefit you to have more, in light of your expectation that tax rates will rise?

- Do you have a source of money, outside of your retirement account, that you can use to pay the taxes that will be due upon the conversion? Is that money that you believe you should be putting to better use or can it be used for the conversion?

- Do you have a reasonably long life expectancy? Do you have children or other heirs to whom you would wish to leave money in a tax-free account? Is it your desire to pay taxes up front to relieve them of that responsibility if they inherit the money someday?

If your answers to many of those questions generally are yes, a conversion to a Roth IRA might make sense for you. In the real world, however, when I explain the conversion concept to people, they often agree that it makes sense—but when it comes time to pay the IRS for the up-front taxes, they hesitate when they find out how much is due. In fact, they almost fall out of their chairs. Conceptually, it makes sense to them. Practically, it's not easy to write that check to Uncle Sam. It's like losing weight. Sure, it sounds like a great idea, but that treadmill seems so intimidating.

YOUR FAIR SHARE

We all must pay our fair share of taxes, but nothing is unethical about using the tax laws to your best advantage and saving where possible. As long as you are proceeding legally, it is your right to avail yourself of whatever tax breaks you can get. The government, in fact, has incorporated those breaks into the tax code for very good reasons. It is in the public interest to promote and encourage certain behaviors, such as owning a home and contributing to charity.

However, nobody is going to come knocking at your door to tell you about those breaks. Nobody from the IRS will be showing up to tutor you. Likewise, stockbrokers are unlikely to be offering you useful tax advice; they may be trying to maximize the potential rate of return, but they do not think about the tax ramifications.

This is a case of "let the buyer beware." The individual citizen is expected to stay informed and up-to-date with the tax rules—and since that is quite a daunting task, many people choose to work with CPAs and financial planners who are familiar with the range of opportunities at their disposal.

When it comes to saving on taxes, you need to look beyond the moment for a view of how today's decisions will influence you in the years ahead. Tax management is a key function of thorough financial planning for retirement, and it has been my privilege to serve as a guide for many families.

CHAPTER 9

BUCKETS OF INCOME

Of primary concern to virtually all retirees is where they will be getting the income to see them through the years ahead—a period of time that could well be as long as they spent earning a paycheck. What will replace that regular salary, now that their working years are over? It's a big question both for multimillionaires and for those with a more modest portfolio. Each has the same objective—continuing their accustomed lifestyle into retirement.

In the previous chapter, we took a look at three "buckets" for tax management, and those carry significant implications for retirement income planning as well. In this chapter, we will look at three other buckets that represent investment and cash flow for retirement. These are the buckets for short-term spending, mid-term spending, and long-term spending. As with the tax buckets, each will be filled with different types of investments. These represent that third leg of the stool for retirement planning, the one that is taken on such major importance in this post-pension era.[10]

---

10   Voya Services Company, *Financial Strategies for Successful Retirement* [seminar and workbook], 2017.

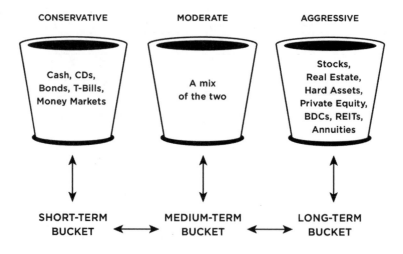

The aim is to generate the money that you will need to meet your desired standard of living and to do so while keeping risk as low as possible to produce the necessary results. Of course, you will need first to identify that desired standard of living—and that is why we have discussed at length the need to set clear and practical life goals. Only then can you take a hard look at the right investment choices to cover both essential needs and lifelong dreams.

The bucket system helps people to visualize the importance of proper asset allocation. As my son Ethan is a visual learner, I can totally associate with the trait. In the long-term bucket will be investments that can be somewhat more aggressive because the money will not be needed for a good while. In the mid-term bucket, the investments will tend to be more moderate because they likely will be tapped within several years. And in the short-term bucket, the investments will be conservative. That money will be needed for immediate expenses and for potential emergencies, and therefore it must be secure and accessible. It should be kept away from risk.

Thinking in terms of those buckets is a form of mental accounting that works well for many people. You could empty those three buckets into one big bucket, mixing the safe, moderate, and aggressive investments all together, and the results would be relatively moderate. However, it helps to divvy them up into those separate buckets for clarity regarding taxation, spending, and distribution. People who are fundamentally risk averse will feel the reassurance that they will not be pouring anything out of that long-term bucket for a decade or more, and in the meantime they have their other two buckets where the money is at lesser risk.

In effect, the bucket system helps people to think in terms of time horizon and risk tolerance in a way that would be harder to see if the money were lumped together. Should the money actually be in separate accounts? Some prefer it that way. They like to watch the differing performances, and it makes rebalancing easier. If the market should fall and reduce the value of holdings in the long-term bucket, they like to see that the short-term and mid-term buckets have held their own by comparison. They find comfort in that clarity. Other investors prefer to just pour the buckets together, so to speak, knowing that on the whole they are investing moderately with some conservative assets and some that are more aggressive. I can accommodate either investment model among my clients.

Again, it comes down to the concept of asset allocation. Often you will see a pie chart in which the various asset classes are divided. The pie includes short-term, mid-term, and long-term assets as segments of the allocation. That chart could easily be redrawn as three pies, or buckets, one conservative, one moderate, and one more aggressive.

WHAT'S YOUR FIGURE?

Over the years, various economists, actuaries, and other theorists have weighed in on the percentage that could reasonably be withdrawn annually from a retirement account without severely eroding the principal. One such figure is 4 percent, as discussed in a previous chapter, and many financial planners consider that appropriate. Some suggest higher. I have seen studies that put it as low as 2 or 3 percent, particularly in the low interest rate environment that we have been experiencing.

Many people dramatically overestimate how much they can withdraw from their account and sustain it. I have heard people suggest they can take out 8 to 10 percent for their retirement living expenses. They simply do not understand the danger they are posing to their portfolio. In the 1980s and 1990s, and even in the early 2000s, interest rates were higher and money market accounts and CDs paid a return of several percent. Back then somewhat higher portfolio withdrawal rates were more realistic. It's simply not the case when interest rates are barely above zero, with historically low inflation and tax rates. It's highly unlikely that you could withdraw 10 percent from an account and still grow it and sustain the principal. Meanwhile, portfolios must meet the demands of increasingly long life expectancies. That, too, calls for a lower withdrawal rate.

Four percent is the traditional starting point, but without the ability to predict the future, the appropriate withdrawal rate is just a guess. We do not know where inflation and taxes will be. We do not know what interest rates will be. We cannot say how investments will perform. Goals and dreams and spending habits change. No individual knows his or her exact life expectancy. Illness strikes, and people pass away. The contingencies are countless—and that is why a thorough financial plan is so important.

The goal is now to develop a lifetime income. I think that's been a general shift in attitude over the past decade or so. The paradigm has shifted. The dollar amount is seen as less significant now than the income stream that you need when you retire. It is no longer "I need $3 million." Now it is "I need $80,000 a year."

That has become the new retirement vision for a great many people. They are not working toward a lump sum. They are working toward a regular and reliable income. They want to make sure that they will have sufficient money for the rest of their lives to cover their base expenses and then the discretionary money to go after their dreams. I have heard it called a paycheck and a playcheck.

All the while, they need to build enough value to overcome inflation, keeping in mind that it might not always be as tame as it has been in recent years. Even at a typical and steady rate of inflation at 3 percent, an income of $100,000 today would have to rise to about $210,000 in twenty-five years to command the same purchasing power. Compare today's prices with what you paid many years ago—the price of a house or a car, for example, or a loaf of bread, or a gallon of gas, or a postage stamp. The "rule of 72"[11] is an easy formula to estimate how long it will take for prices in general to double. Investors often use that same formula to figure how many years it will take for their money to double at a given annual rate of return, and the rule also works for gauging inflation. If you divide the rate into 72, the result is the number of years it will take for prices to double. For example, at a steady rate of 3 percent inflation, prices double in twenty-four years ($72 \div 3 = 24$).

---

11   Years required to double investment = 72 ÷ compound annual interest rate

LIQUIDITY, SAFETY, GROWTH

Just as there is danger in pursuing too much growth and taking on excessive risk in the market, so too there is a danger in trying to be too safe. If you keep your money in a bank account or CD, you will not be keeping up with inflation. Neither will you be able to keep up with the increase in taxes. You certainly will not be able to sustain a 4 percent withdrawal rate through such conservative investing. This relates back to the loanership versus ownership discussion. As we have seen, too aggressive a stance invokes the risk of market loss and falling victim to the sequence of returns, which can devastate the retirement portfolio. You need to find a way to strike the right balance for you. You need a combination of liquidity, safety, and growth in a portfolio if you expect it to last throughout the years of your retirement.

Many people are eager for liquidity in their investments, but often they are getting that at the expense of the safety and growth. Likewise, to get growth you may need to sacrifice a degree of liquidity and safety. If you want safety, you likely should expect less growth. Just as I would not recommend that anyone put all their assets into a CD, I certainly wouldn't recommend that anyone retire with all their assets in the stock market. Sanity lies somewhere between those two.

Think of the largest assets that the average American owns. The biggest asset, as I pointed out earlier, is the ability to produce income, but in specific terms the top three tend to be: 1) the equity in a house; 2) a retirement account; and 3) the cash value and death benefit in a life insurance policy. What those three have in common is that they are, for the most part, illiquid. It's not money that you can easily raid. In addition, each of them also represents forced savings. You have to pay your mortgage every month or you lose your house. Typically, your retirement account contributions come out of your paycheck automatically. And to avoid losing your life insurance policy, you must pay that bill and make that contribution regularly.

None of those three major assets is a ready source of liquid money—nor should it be. Liquidity is not always desirable. It simply has its proper place. In the bucket system, you would put the liquid money in the short-term one. Safe money also would be in there and in the mid-term bucket as well. The mid-term bucket would also have some growth money, but most of that would be in the long-term bucket.

Each financial solution has been designed for a specific use. You have investments for every purpose. In a balanced income plan, those solutions will be in their proper place, delivering the results that they were meant to deliver. Some might be producing a guaranteed income, while others are building growth as an inflation buffer. Some will entail an element of risk, and some will be providing you with a sense of stability and security. Some will provide money for now, some will provide money for later. Only you and your family can determine the sensible balance for your life and for your retirement.

BEYOND THE BUCKETS

Nobody knows exactly how much money they will need when they retire. Determining a retirement income is an inexact science in which you and your advisor must size up your goals, needs, essential assets, and other resources. Then we take into consideration inflation and risk tolerances. We look for the balance between a realistic rate of return and a realistic withdrawal rate. Beyond that, it's a long and winding road into and through retirement, but you must plan based on the information you have currently available and on your best projections of what is likely to be. That's the best that we can do.

Those three buckets of retirement income planning will likely be sufficient to get you and your spouse through your retirement. In fact, the third bucket, which functions for the long term, may still be fairly full upon your passing—meaning that it could spill over into what amounts to a fourth one. You might call it the *legacy bucket*. It's the money that you will be leaving to your loved ones and other heirs.

We have talked about the accumulation and the distribution phases of life. For many, there is a third phase, the legacy phase. This is the planning that extends beyond your lifetime, and it is measured in terms not only of money but also of values and dreams. This is the planning that reaches for posterity. This is how we pay it forward. I love this quote from Winston Churchill. He said, "We make a living by what we get. We make a life by what we give." In my final chapter, let's conclude by talking about the legacy you plan to leave behind.

CHAPTER 10

PLANNING FOR POSTERITY

By default, you have an estate plan. If you have not taken action on your own to settle your affairs, then you can be sure that the government will do that for you. If you have not determined what will become of all of your possessions and your life's work, then your state will step in with its judicial powers to get things in order for you. Unfortunately, you might not agree with what the judge and the lawyers have to say.

The primary aim of estate planning is to determine how your life's work will be managed if you die or become unable to handle your own affairs. Most people care deeply about how those resources will be passed on to loved ones. They want the property and the money to go to the people they choose, and they want to decide how and when that will happen. They may wish to apportion some of their wealth to charity. They wish this all to be done with tax efficiency and without getting the courts unduly involved in private family matters. Probate can be messy, sometimes costly, and it can seem to drag on endlessly.

Despite these important considerations, I have had clients tell me that they don't much care what happens to their stuff after they are gone and that they do not wish to talk about it because as soon as they do, they will drop dead. You might say that is taking Murphy's

Law to a bit of an extreme, but it does illustrate the great reluctance that many people feel regarding estate planning.

Certainly it is unpleasant to contemplate your own demise, and that of course is the premise whenever the talk turns to such topics as long-term-care planning and gifting assets to children. Estate planning by its nature seems to inspire procrastination, which we already have identified as the greatest threat to retirement security. It is also the greatest threat to sensibly transitioning assets to the next generation. You spend decades building an estate and acquiring property, investments, business interests, and other resources. That's a lot to sacrifice just because it's hard to talk about dying, which you can be sure is something that you one day will do.

You can think of your last will and testament as your opportunity to put finishing touches on your financial plan. You are establishing continuity into the next generation. You are writing the final chapter of your life's achievements, and you should want to write it well. Instead of ceding to the government such important decisions as who will get your assets, why not take the time to make sure that your life's work goes to those you most trust and whom deserve it?

THE PASSING OF ASSETS

The will is an important document, but it does not stand alone. Many times people are confused about what it actually does. They may think that it has the ultimate power to direct where all of the assets go, and that might not be the case at all.

There are three primary means by which assets are passed on. The first way is through "operation of law," usually via a beneficiary designation. Whenever assets have a named beneficiary, whether that's an IRA or 401(k) or other investment account or life insurance policy, they go directly to that person. That transfer of assets is not governed by the will and will not need to go through probate. Much of a person's net worth may be in the form of assets and investments with beneficiaries.

Another way that assets are transferred is through joint ownership, which is another form of operation of law. If an account is owned jointly, as with a child or a spouse, that person will automatically take over that account. This transfer, too, takes place outside of any provisions in the will and is not subjected to probate.

Trusts of various kinds are the third common means of asset transfer. They come in an assortment of varieties—revocable or irrevocable, testamentary and living, incentive and bypass, special needs and irrevocable life insurance trusts, as a few examples. Each has a specific function to fill a particular need and planning scenario. For the most part, anything placed in a trust will not go through the will or the probate process.

Unless your assets are in one of those three categories, there will be a good chance that their disposition will be governed by your will or be determined by the courts through probate. A well-orchestrated estate plan can avoid that outcome.

A PYRAMID OF PRIORITIES

You might think of the estate planning process as a pyramid. At its base are the assets that have beneficiary designations and that are held in joint ownership. The next level up would be the simple will, along with powers of attorney for financial and health-care decisions, and an advance medical directive, often called a living will. Higher on the pyramid would be the various types of trusts, topped by increasingly advanced planning strategies, such as family limited partnerships and charitable remainder trusts.

ESTATE PLANNING PYRAMID

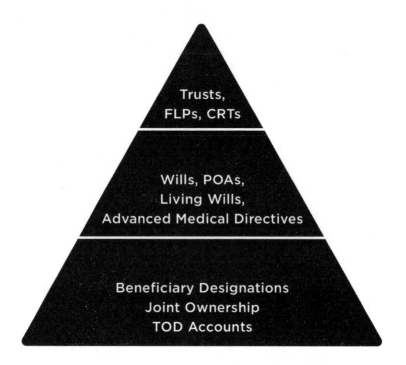

In working with clients, we can climb that pyramid[12] as high as necessary to accomplish their goals for estate planning. Many families do not need the higher levels, but estate planning includes mechanisms for a wide variety of circumstances. Some are exceedingly complicated, and I can help my clients see through the complexities and guide them to the level of professional assistance that will serve them best.

---

12   Voya Services Company, *Financial Strategies for Successful Retirement* [seminar and workbook], 2017.

The fundamentals, however, must be in place. Those powers of attorney are essential. Let's say a husband and wife own property together and the wife becomes incapacitated. Without her signature, it will be very difficult for the husband to sell the property if need be. He would have to go to court and take the matter in front of a judge. A durable power of attorney avoids that problem. Likewise, the health care power of attorney authorizes medical decisions. A living will also should be among the estate planning documents. If you were on life support and unable to express your preferences, would you want the doctors to "pull the plug"? Many people wish to express those preferences in advance, and the proper documentation will direct the decision based on your desires, not someone else's. You might feel that your spouse would do what was best—but without a living will, he or she lacks that legal power.

You have a lot of options in your estate planning, just as you do in your investing. Some people try the do-it-yourself approach to their finances, trying to handle matters by what they have learned from television or magazines. Others consult with qualified financial professionals. Likewise, some people's idea of estate planning is to download documents from a website. Some people jot down some things on a paper napkin and ask someone to sign, date, and witness it. They expect that to satisfy legal requirements. Maybe, or maybe not.

Remember that estate planning represents your best efforts for the end of your journey. You should do it right. This is no place to count nickels and dimes. A few hundred dollars spent to meet with a qualified attorney could pay major dividends. You need to get your priorities in place if you are to complete your journey at the destination of your choosing.

15 QUESTIONS TO CONSIDER
BEFORE PREPARING YOUR WILL

1. Who will be the executor of your will?

If you are married, your primary executor is typically your spouse. Other primary or successor executor options might be one child, all of your children together, a sibling, etc., or a bank/trust company, which can be named in case of a common disaster (all immediate family members die before your estate is distributed).

2. Will you use a "bypass trust" to save taxes?

If you are married, an advantage of using a bypass trust is that it passes assets estate tax-free to your heirs immediately upon the passing of the last spouse. One disadvantage is that while your spouse can be a trustee of his/her own trust, you must have a co-trustee to decide on any encroachments on principal for the benefit of a spouse.

3. When you die (or if married, when the last spouse dies), will your estate go directly to your children/beneficiaries, or will you use a trust? If you use a trust, who will be designated as the trustee?

If considering an individual as trustee, consider naming two for accountability, and specify who will be the successor trustee if one trustee fails to serve.

4. If you use a trust (whether a living or a testamentary trust), when will the children/benefi-

ciaries be entitled to receive the principal of the trust?

You could choose to have them receive it all at a certain age (for example, age twenty-five) or stagger the payments (for example, ages twenty-five, thirty, and thirty-five).

5. If you have children, will you treat them differently in your will?

Some of your children may have greater financial burdens, such as a child with special needs. You may have children who have not used good judgment in choosing a marriage partner, or children who are "spendthrifts" for whom you may want to continue the trust for life.

6. Will you put special provisions in your will for your grandchildren?

One thing to consider is if you will undermine your children's authority over their children by leaving a large inheritance to your grandchildren. If you do leave your grandchildren an inheritance, you may want to use an educational trust to help them with college, or stipulate requirements before they receive their inheritance, such as taking a mission trip or finishing college. Most importantly, give your grandchildren clear instructions on what it is you feel is intended for the use of these assets.

7. Will you include charitable giving in your will?

Have you considered including a bequest for those charities you have faithfully supported during your lifetime? Have you also considered the use of a charitable remainder trust, charitable lead trust, or charitable gift annuity? Or establishing a private foundation, supporting organization or donor-advised fund?

8. Will you fund a charitable giving vehicle in your will (e.g., a private foundation, donor-advised fund, or supporting organization)?

A giving vehicle such as the ones listed here can help you execute your stewardship responsibility in a strategic and systematic fashion even after your death.

9. Who will you name as guardians of your minor children in your will?

Don't name a couple if you only want one of them to serve, and be sure to name a successor. Don't count out a generation above you. Naming your parents could be a smart option.

10. How will you handle the disposition of your closely held business?

Is there a buy-sell arrangement with your partners or co-shareholders? Does the life insurance funding the buy-sell go to an escrow agent, your partner, or the business? If it goes to the business, be aware of the possibility of your partner keeping the proceeds, or the company using it to pay creditors. Do you have children receiving stock who are not involved in the company? Watch out for family problems that such an arrangement can cause. Is the right child in control of the business, or would it be better to have a committee of your children involved? Should you establish an independent board of directors to run the business for a time after your death? If you are leaving the stock to your spouse, is she or he prepared to handle the tough decisions, or do you need to make other arrangements?

11. Do you need to deal with children from a prior marriage?

Not doing so may cause severe problems for your spouse after your death and create hard feelings among your children.

12. Do you have a method of distributing items of personal property or heirlooms in order to avoid a family fight? Have you already had conversations with family members so that this is not surprising at your death?

Many states legally permit you to incorporate the provisions of a separate letter into your will so you can clearly identify your intended distribution of these items, and if you later change your mind, you only need to change the letter (and not your will).

13. Do you have a plan in the event of a common disaster (all family members die at once)?

Many people list their church and favorite ministries as successor beneficiaries in the event of a common disaster.

14. Will your spouse know what your assets and liabilities are after your death?

One wise thing to do is to keep one file drawer at home dedicated solely to assets, and one to liabilities, and show your spouse where they are now.

Make sure your spouse knows where all personal vital documents are stored and how to access them.

15. Do you have unique circumstances that might require special provisions in your will, such as a QTIP trust, a QDOT trust, generation skipping provisions, personal residence trusts, and family limited partnerships?

These are separate issues which you should thoroughly discuss with your professional advisor before making decisions, as they can have severe ramifications for your spouse and family.

Supplied by RICK | LINN, LLC (http://www.ricklinn.com).

PROFESSIONAL GUIDANCE

You might wonder why you should go to the trouble of having an attorney set up a trust, as opposed to a simple will. Besides the ability to keep assets out of probate, and besides a variety of potential tax advantages, there is this fundamental function of a trust that makes it highly valuable in estate planning. It gives you, in essence, the ability to continue doing what is best for your family, even after you have passed away. You can continue your influence from the grave.

Rather than leaving money to your loved ones upon your death, you can gift money to beneficiaries at certain time periods in their lives, or when they reach certain milestones such as college graduation or marriage or the purchase of a first house. You also can designate trustees to whom you give the authority to decide when and if the child should receive money and how it will be distributed. In many families, the parents are concerned about leaving money to a particular son or daughter who they feel lacks the maturity to manage it well. The trust can be structured so that the money is distributed only in increments and only upon satisfying certain requirements. In other cases, the parents might wish to set up a special distribution to a child with special needs or who likely will require a lifetime of care.

I have seen a wide range of issues that so many families face. Generally, the need for further estate planning arises when we uncover situations as we review the finances and retirement goals. As we discuss family issues, the need for a particular type of trust might become quite apparent, and we can talk about solutions that the family might not have thought were possible.

The relationship that I am able to establish with my clients is what allows us to discover those solutions. I have seen what has worked well for others. I get to know the family and the issues, emotions, and family dynamics that are involved. Estate planning often requires the work of an attorney, but together my clients and I can do some of the preliminary work to make that legal consultation as efficient as possible, identifying the major issues in advance.

I can work as a facilitator between the client and the attorney, making sure that all pertinent issues are covered and that my client's needs have been fully expressed and addressed. Whether they are working with their own lawyer or I refer them to one, my job is to make sure that professional does not need to start from scratch. I already understand what my clients are facing and hoping to accomplish, and I can make sure those matters get communicated. I already know their attitude toward money, their family background, how they feel about their children and grandchildren, and their views on leaving money to them. Why should the attorney need to ask all those questions again? I certainly defer to his or her legal expertise, but I know that the attorney appreciates my suggestions as I help to guide the conversation.

LEAVING A LEGACY

Another objective of estate planning is the efficient distribution of money to charity or to a foundation. Instead of the government collecting taxes and distributing your assets as it sees fit, you can maintain control over exactly who will benefit from your life's work.

The question of charitable contributions, however, often is given only cursory attention during financial planning. The matter is reduced to a bullet point on a checklist: "To what extent do you wish to donate money to charitable causes?" For many people, their gut reaction is to say that they already give some money and that they hadn't really thought about it but might consider it at some point. And then they and the planner move on to the next matter at hand. Having gotten to know the family, I already understand what is important to them and their charitable inclinations. That, too, is information that I can communicate as their lawyer proceeds to develop an estate plan.

Estate planning to a large extent might better be called *legacy planning*. It's not only about the money and the taxes. It is about passing along family values and a set of ethics. It's about making sure that the rising generations understand the family mission and vision. That is a bequest more important, I believe, than leaving money and property. That is a gift that endures long after material things have departed. My parents left me a valuable legacy. I think of the life lessons that they instilled in their children and know that those lessons cannot be found in a bank account.

I once rented out the Movie Tavern in nearby Collegeville to show my appreciation to clients by offering them dinner and a show. They were curious as to what the movie would be—the latest blockbuster, perhaps? "No, I'm going to show you something a little different, another kind of adventure," I told them. "It's called *The Ultimate Gift.*"

Spoiler alert here. The movie is about a spoiled brat whose grandfather intends to leave him a fortune. The grandfather, however, places some conditions on the inheritance: the young man must perform a series of tasks. The grandfather calls them "gifts." By meeting those challenges, the young man progressively learns about hard work, charity, and the value of a dollar. He learns also that love is more important than money. And along the way he finds romance with a woman whose daughter is dying of cancer. He becomes a different person, and he inherits the fortune—which he uses to build a hospital and start a foundation in the child's memory.

Many of my clients thanked me for showing that movie—and I could tell that they were not just being polite. "You've been helping us get our financial house organized and have provided valuable advice along the way and things like that," one of them said, "but this really opened our eyes. This is why it matters. We can see what's best to leave our kids and grandkids."

Quite often, my clients tell me that they wish they could tell their story in a book or a video. They want to leave something besides an account with their money in it. They want to leave an accounting of their lives, with their heart in it.

That's really the point of the wills and trusts and all those documents; they are the means to leave something of yourself—a legacy—to your family and to the world. That's the essence of estate planning. And that, after all, is the ultimate aim of financial planning. I'd like to conclude with a quote from Mahatma Ghandi. He said, "The future depends on what we do in the present." I hope this book has inspired you to take the next step toward your dream retirement. Is there an area I touched upon where you are procrastinating or simply need to improve? Take action today and you'll be one step closer to achieving the retirement you deserve.

Do you have a story you'd like to share about how my book has helped you or someone you know? I'd love to hear from you at thomasakalejta@gmail.com.

YOUR TRUE NET WORTH

Financial education and advocacy have been the priorities of my career. I learned valuable lessons handed down in my own family, and my mission became helping others do the best they can by avoiding the big mistakes that set back so many families. My goal has been to equip people with the knowledge that they need to make the best financial decisions possible.

In the chapters of this book, I have shared much of my philosophy and a variety of the details involved in making those good choices. We have looked at rates of return and tax savings and investment priorities and insurances and an assortment of other concerns. Those are the nuts and bolts of what I do.

When it comes down to it, though, why do I do it? Why do I believe that it is so important that people understand these matters? The slogan and tag line of my firm is this: "Building wealth and protecting dreams." That's what I do. I help people to build their wealth—and why? So that they can rally the resources to pursue those dreams during their retirement years and leave a legacy for their loved ones.

I think of my children. Like all parents, Sue and I want the best for our family. That is why we build. Both our children will pursue their own dreams. Ethan will face special challenges as he makes his way through life, and for that we need a special strength. We are family, and we are here for one another. The goal of most generations is that the children have a better life. So it is with us.

Through the seasons of our lives, we each are writing our eulogy. As people look back on our time on earth, what will they say about you? Will they be nodding solemnly at your funeral as they talk about how much you socked away in your investments or how much you saved in taxes? Or will they be talking about your values? About your spiritual and charitable ways? About your kindness and devotion as a parent?

Your greatest gift is your story. Your loved ones will remember your integrity and your vision. And how can we best protect those dreams? How can we be the good stewards of all that has been given to us? By making the most of our resources in the here and now. By working hard for the harvest to come. Your financial affairs are the building blocks for your dreams—but take care that the money is not the only asset that gets counted. Your net worth encompasses so much more.